2.50

The Budget-Watcher's Cookbook

THE BUDGET-WATCHER'S COOKBOOK

———— ❀ ————

Kay Sullivan

———— ❀ ————

The McCall Publishing Company

NEW YORK

CONTENTS

FOREWORD

Cooking one, two, or three meals a day for 365 days a year with a few vacation days, Mother's Day, and a birthday or anniversary off for good behavior is challenge enough for the homemaker. But having to stick to a budget as well—that's really pushing the lady in the kitchen beyond endurance.

Yet, with the cost of living going in one direction—up—and demands on the family finances multiplying constantly, most homemakers are well aware of the need to keep food expenditures down. Not bread-and-water down, you understand, but certainly no daily menus of caviar and squab. Contemporary custom seems to decree that smart housewives must be prepared and able to serve Cordon Bleu meals on shoestring budgets. What's more, the family must never suspect. Never should there be the slightest suspicion that a meal is anything but expressly chosen and cooked to please the most demanding family palate. No one must know about the special on flank steak, the day-old bread in the custard, the substitute for pure olive oil in the salad dressing.

If you are determined to eat well and yet not spend a lot of money on food, you must face the fact that your time is going to replace your money. Inexpensive meals that are truly appealing are seldom prepared in a jiffy. They require thought, patience, and planning. It takes courage, stamina, and know-how to triumph over the high cost of food and meet the challenge of budget cookery. Not everyone can do it alone. That's why there are so many penny-wise cookbooks on the market, all aimed at telling the shopper how to get the most for her money in the market place. And how to cook and serve her bargains so they do not betray their economical sources.

The Budget-Watcher's Cookbook is in this category but it has a distinct difference. No attempt has been made to review all the basic routines of food preparation. We assume the reader knows how to boil water, fry a frankfurter, scrape a carrot. Or if she doesn't, we know there are dozens of how-to-cook cookbooks that can instruct her in the fundamentals.

What we have attempted is to acknowledge the plight of today's housewife who, in addition to being talented, adept, and ingenious in front of the stove, must also be thrifty, and we have provided her with helpful guidelines for selecting and preparing appetizing economical foods. The recipes included in this book have been tested in the Hunt-Wesson Kitchens or in the author's home. There may be some who will question the mathematical balance of our selection—twenty-five ways to prepare hamburger, for example, and only one for liver! Our rationale is simple: people eat hamburger much more often than they do liver—we figure about twenty-five times to one. And hamburger is more economical.

If you notice the prevalence of tomatoes in one form or another in many main dishes, there is a reason for that, too. Tomatoes are the cosmetics of the economy cuisine; they can make any dish look and taste good. If that is not reason enough, it so happens that the man in our house likes tomatoes. In fact, as far as he is concerned, we have never had a failure with anything containing tomatoes (except for a tomato-colored birthday tie that went right to the back of the closet and stayed there).

For the hesitant homemaker, we bring assurance. The problem of keeping within a food budget can be solved. It is much like losing weight. It takes motivation, determination, and a sense of timing. You cannot put it off until tomorrow. You must start now.

So start reading . . . and pick a recipe or two from among the 350 herein for your very next meal. Soon, with the money you save, you may be able to buy another copy of *The Budget-Watcher's Cookbook* for an extravagant friend.

KAY SULLIVAN

The Budget-Watcher's Cookbook

INTRODUCTION

Words for the Thrifty Food Shopper

Every homemaker about to embark on a food shopping expedition must have a bit of the Girl Scout in her—namely, she must "Be prepared." A Prudence Penny never sails into a supermarket and grabs wildly at whatever meets her eye. *She* has a shopping list—and before the list, she has a budget.

How to arrive at a food budget? Be a tape-saver for a month, and you will have the answers. Tape-savers are shoppers who take home and do not throw away that little strip of paper with figures on it given to them by the cashier at the check-out counter. Accumulate the slips long enough to see just how much you have been spending on food. It is easier to cut down on food expenses if you know the sums you have been spending. If you loathe figures, do not struggle to be too precise. Stay with it long enough to make a rough estimate of what you usually expend to keep you and your family happily well fed, then keep within that amount if it is a reasonable figure. Do not forget to add in the money for the milkman, egg man, and bread man, if you use such services. And beware of the temptation to let these men drop off extra items you do not really need.

Before you put a foot out the door to go shopping, you must do some other preparatory work. First, check the newspaper ads to see what meats, vegetables, and fruits are plentiful and specially priced. (Advertised specials are often based on the list of plentiful foods issued to grocers by the United States Department of Agriculture.) Secondly, with this information in mind, plan your menus for the next few days or the week and make a list of all the items you will need to prepare those menus. Include snacks, too. Finally, check the refrigerator, freezer, and pantry shelves to see what you already have on hand. In that way you can avoid buying doubles when there is no need to.

List in hand, you now are ready to head for the market. Try to do your shopping early in the day so you can get first dibs on the specials. Also, you will find that the fruits and vegetables are fresher in the morning and not yet pinched and picked over by an army of your peers.

Incidentally, it is wise to shop in a supermarket for staples, canned goods, and frozen items. Chain stores are able to offer better prices and a wider variety of brands and sizes than the independent grocer. However, you may want to remain loyal to your independent market for meats and fresh vegetables. There is absolutely no question that a cook's best friend is her butcher—providing she has carefully flattered and cajoled him over the months into thinking he is unique and that only she really appreciates his talents. (She can be sure she's made her point when he saves her the leanest bacon, the thickest steaks, and even makes her a crown roast without grumbling.)

We strongly recommend going on all food shopping expeditions alone. Well, a child or two may be a necessity, and picking up the stuff they throw out of the shopping cart can be counted as good exercise for the hips. We would not suggest taking along a neighbor or a husband. Consciously or unconsciously, you are going to try to impress the neighbor by buying a higher priced item or an extra item you do not need. If she squeals in delight over the canned brandied pears and puts two in her basket, you're not going to spoil the fun. Pinchpenny, yes; spoilsport, never. Therefore, one can of brandied pears goes into your basket. As for your husband—any husband—the sooner you recognize the fact that men are all secret members of SATES (Supermarket Association to Encourage Squandering), the better.

It is totally impossible to take a husband into a market and escape without spending twice what you planned. He will head straight for the gourmet shelf and grab several cans and jars of delicacies you would not buy even for a visiting rich uncle. At the fresh fruit counter, just watch. He will reach for the pomegranates, Persian melon, and hothouse grapes. And letting him within range of meats is a disaster. He will never notice a chicken wing or a ham hock—but, oh, that porterhouse steak!

So there you are, alone in a supermarket, early in the morning, and armed with your shopping list. All you have to control are your own burning desires to cut loose and buy the thick cream and the strawberries, the *filet mignon,* and the *pâté de foie gras.* Shall we tell you what a friend of ours does to hold down these spendthrift urges? She never trundles out a shopping cart without affixing a red plastic clothespin to the front of it. It's her private storm warning. It signals: Don't buy it if you don't need it and watch the price. Try it—it can work for you. Just make certain you remove the clothespin at the check-out counter or you may eventually be in trouble when you go to hang out the wash.

How to Turn a Food Shopping Expedition into a Budgetary Triumph

On the supermarket battlefront, the homemaker can be the victor. If she reads her newspaper ads carefully and follows the weekly price wars, she can save as much as 25 percent or more on many items. By purchasing specials in quantity, she will make considerable savings for future food bills and, also, make her freezer pay for itself. She should buy graded merchandise—meats, poultry, butter, eggs, and canned goods—for the purpose it will serve: highest grades for occasions when perfect appearance and top quality are desired; medium grades for everyday use; lower grades for thrift and when appearance is not all-important. And certainly she should recognize the fact that ready-to-eat foods such as cooked meats, salads, and bakery goods are going to be more expensive than the same items prepared at home because their cost includes a charge for time and labor, as well as the price of the food itself.

Here are some specific guidelines for economical shopping.

1. Keep your shopping list flexible. You may plan to buy beef, get to the store, and find a nonadvertised special on pork that is a better buy. Be pliant enough to change your mind and your menu. You'll save money if you do.

2. Meat, fish, and poultry account for 35 percent of all food spending: Watch for sales on this trio and you'll make significant savings.

3. Buy what you need, not what attracts your eye or tempts your taste buds. When buying fruits and vegetables, for example, take

home only what you can consume. Nothing is more spendthrift than throwing out overripe, unused food.

4. In the same vein, bring along coupons or discount slips but use only the ones that fit your family needs. There is not much sense in buying frozen okra at fifteen cents off if nobody in the family likes okra.

5. Compare private label brands with nationally advertised brands. You may be able to save considerably by choosing the private label. A one-pound package of margarine under a private label, for example, will sell for much less than the nationally advertised brands.

6. Watch for "twofers" and do not break up the sets. When an item is priced "two for something," you will save pennies at least by buying both.

7. Take advantage of seasonal foods. Fresh fruits and vegetables in season are usually cheaper than the frozen or canned variety. The exception to this rule is orange juice concentrate, which is normally lower in price than the freshly squeezed variety.

8. Always check the price per unit weight of a giant "economy-size" package to be sure it really is the buy it is supposed to be. Sometimes a smaller size will be cheaper. And bargain or not, there's no use in buying the giant size of something if you are not going to use it all. If it makes more sense to buy a smaller size, do so.

9. Do buy the large packages of dry cereals—those individual little boxes may be convenient but they cost much more per serving. The same is true of raisins. Skip those costly miniature boxes and buy the large box; make up your own lunch box raisin packets in plastic bags.

10. Eggs can save money for you if you compare the cost of the various sizes. Medium eggs are less expensive than large ones; brown eggs may cost less than white ones and the color does not affect the quality.

11. If you use a lot of fresh milk, buy half-gallon containers at the supermarket, thereby eliminating costly home deliveries. Powdered skim milk is usually one of the best buys among supermarket weekend specials; you can save at least one third on its price. Condensed and evaporated milk can also be thrifty buys, and, used in cooking and baking, they are real cost-cutters.

12. You are no doubt aware (after all those TV ads) that margarine is the lower-priced spread. But do you know that butter by the pound is less expensive than butter divided into quarter-pound wrapped sticks?

13. If you don't mind changing tea brands, there's always some brand with a special offer on tea bags. Keep in mind that tea bags and instant tea are more expensive than loose tea. Instant coffee, on the other hand, is a more economical buy than fresh ground.

14. Recognize that salad dressings, mayonnaise, many canned and condensed soups and sauces (especially tomato), seasonings, pudding and dessert mixes, biscuit, cake and pie-crust mixes, and packaged cookies are usually cheaper than making these products from scratch, when cost is compared to the value of time spent in preparing the dishes completely.

15. Other relatively inexpensive foods that make wise buys include: canned fish, such as tuna; pork and beans; peanut butter; frankfurters; long-cooking cereals; some canned fruit juices; frozen fish fillets; rice, macaroni, and spaghetti; some canned fruits and vegetables, and some frozen vegetables, especially peas and spinach.

16. Order bulk foods by weight rather than by volume or number when possible. It is simpler to compare the price of lemons in two stores, for example, when the price is given by the pound rather than the dozen since a dozen lemons may include fruit ranging greatly in size.

17. If you live in a one-room apartment, forget it, but if you have plenty of storage space, buy on-sale staples and canned food by the case. Do this only with items you use regularly, such as canned soup or pet foods.

18. Don't scoot by the day-old baked goods counter. Day-old breads and some cakes are often sold at half the original price and they are quite usable for toasting, stuffings, and bread puddings. Commercial breads freeze well and may be stored in a freezer up to three months, so buy and stock up when the price is right.

19. Before you wheel up to the check-out counter, look in that bulging basket, see if there's one item there that you don't really need, and PUT IT BACK.

Feeding the Kitchen Piggy Bank

If you are seriously determined to stretch your food dollars, you must realize that not all the stretching takes place in the supermarket—a lot can happen back in your own kitchen. There are innumerable ways to economize in food preparation. Some are common knowledge—like saving bacon drippings for use in cooking. Others may come as a surprise to you. Even if they sound miserly, try them. They may well be worthwhile. An English poet once wrote, "The back door robs the house"; and you know where the back door usually is—right off the kitchen.

Leftovers. Make the most of leftovers but do so attractively. Nobody wants to face a dab of dried-out meat or vegetable for dinner, but if you put some thought and energy into the task, you will discover many interesting dishes that will transform your leftovers into an appetizing second meal. Always cool and store leftovers in tightly closed containers to prevent drying out and absorbing other odors in the refrigerator. Put them in the refrigerator immediately and use as soon as possible. Leftover leftovers don't exist in the thrifty cook's household.

Breads and Cakes. Leftover muffins, biscuits, and shortcakes may be freshened successfully if sprinkled lightly with water, placed in a paper bag (snugly closed), and heated in a moderate oven until the crusts are crisp and they are heated through. Or split and toast them under the broiler or in a hot oven.

Stale bread, even when quite hard and old, may still be used for toast; or it may be placed in a slow oven, dried out until hard and crisp, then rolled to form crumbs. Store the crumbs in a jar with a perforated top. Slightly stale bread is fine in bread puddings, scalloped tomatoes, and in stuffings for meat or poultry.

If yours is one of those rare households where cake is occasionally left over, don't feed it to the birds. It can be the basis of a delicious dessert pudding. Cut away the frosting and filling, cube the cake, and combine it with some kind of sauce, such as a lemon sauce. Or slice it and combine with ice cream for a "sandwich" dessert, topped with chocolate syrup.

Milk. Canned and dried milk used in cooking and baking is most economical. Use powdered skim milk in recipes that call for whole milk. Make up for lost fat and calorie content by adding butter or margarine, 1¼ ounces for each quart. Even with this addition, the cost will be much lower than if you use fresh whole milk. Save on your cream bill by diluting evaporated milk with only one part water instead of the usual two parts water; it will have a creamy taste. If you are big milk users, buy the largest size container at your market, no matter if it is a struggle to hoist it into the shopping cart. Avoid single quarts; they cost pennies more. And avoid home-delivered milk if you can—there is always the temptation to let the milkman leave costly "extras."

Eggs. Use small or medium-sized eggs for baking and for making scrambled eggs and sauces. Save the more expensive large or jumbo sizes for frying or poaching when appearance counts. Don't discard leftover egg yolks or egg whites; they can be used in salads, tossed with the greens before adding French dressing, and to glaze bread or rolls or to coat fried foods. Egg yolks poached, then riced, make an attractive garnish. If you know you are going to have several eggs left over at the week's end, hard-boil them. In that way you can safely keep them for later use and not have them go to waste.

Butter. Grade AA and Grade A butter are superior, but Grade B butter, generally made from selected sour cream, is a thrifty choice for both table and cooking. Actually, it is preferred by some consumers. Butter not intended for use within a few days may be frozen. Frozen butter maintains its quality for two months. It is a good idea to serve butter in pats at the table, so that the younger butter-lovers don't cut off more than they can use. And, of course, margarine is an adequate and thrifty substitute for butter.

Meats. One of the chief ways to save money on meats is knowing how to cook them properly. All meat shrinks to some degree in cooking; to minimize that shrinkage, it should be cooked slowly at a medium temperature. Quick cooking at high temperatures causes excessive shrinkage which means not only loss of flavor, tenderness, and nutritional values but fewer servings as well. Keep in mind, too, that it is economical and a saving on fuel as well to cook certain cuts of meat, such as roasts, in larger quantities than are needed for one meal. If you plan your week's menus ahead, you'll realize how thrifty and time-saving this procedure can be.

Vegetables and Fruits. Cook vegetables and fruits in the shortest possible cooking time to preserve their vitamins and minerals and to get the most and prettiest looking servings. Whenever possible, cook them whole with their outside covering. When paring a vegetable or fruit, always pare as thinly as you can. Do not ever throw away fruit juices or the liquids in which vegetables have been cooked. Canned fruit juices, left after draining fruit, may be used instead of water in making fruit gelatins; combined with water or ginger ale and lemon juice as a beverage; mixed with milk for a children's lunch treat; thickened with cornstarch and used as a sauce on leftover cake; or mixed with mayonnaise to serve over fruit salad. Cook dried fruits and beans in the water in which they have been soaked. Liquids in which vegetables have been cooked, or the reduced liquid from canned vegetables, can be added to soups or used in making white, cream, or cheese sauces to serve with vegetables.

A final suggestion. Get a notebook and start your own collection of unusual ways to save pennies for that kitchen piggy bank. For starters, here are six.

1. Combine jelly left in jars, melt it, and use as a glaze for ham or pour it over fruit tarts.

2. Make your own flavored vinegar for salad dressings by immersing herbs, such as tarragon, and seasonings in plain vinegar until the preferred flavor is obtained. Then strain through a fine cloth, bottle, and cork tightly.

3. Use the ends and pieces, cuts, or slab bacon instead of fancy packaged bacon for sandwiches or in recipes where looks do not count.

4. When using maraschino cherries or olives for garnishing, do not use them whole; get twice as much mileage from a jar by cutting them in half.

5. Instead of buying cubed beef for stewing, buy beef chuck and cube it yourself at home.

6. When a recipe says to brown meat, brown it in the fat trimmed from the meat itself, rather than in butter or other fat.

SOUPS

It is odd how many words that indicate thriftiness begin with "s"—scrimp, stint, skimp, save, scrape, sparing. And then there's "soup."

The cook with an eye on her pocketbook *and* a hungry family counts soup her secret weapon. Whether she makes her own soup from scratch or buys one of the excellent canned, frozen, or dehydrated soups on the market, she can be certain of getting the meal off to a happy, filling—and economical—start.

Years ago it was the accepted custom to keep a soup pot sitting on the stove all the time. If we can believe what we read, apparently everything was tossed into it—bones, bits of meat, leftover vegetables, gravies, and meat juices—and there the pot simmered, filling the kitchen with a savory fragrance and the cook with a sense of self-satisfaction. With her catchall soup pot a-simmering, she wasn't wasting a thing.

Not many homemakers use this frugal technique today. Their soup adventures usually take the form of adding a can of water to a can of concentrated soup or combining two different varieties and gaining a new taste sensation. Even so, they recognize soup for its versatility. It can be the start of a great meal. Or the meal itself. It goes with sandwiches and salads. Served piping hot or icy cold, it fits a winter day or a summer one. Kids and grandfathers like it. Dieters and invalids welcome it. Visitors can be impressed by it ("Didn't you love the way she served the madrilene in blue china teacups?"). What more could a meal planner want?

It is also true that five of the basic canned soups—tomato, consommé, chicken, vegetable, and clam chowder—can serve as the foundation of no less than one hundred different soups. And several soups, like cream of mushroom, celery, or chicken, beef bouillon, and tomato can be used as a basis for sauces and stews galore.

Escoffier, who had a way with a phrase as well as a soup ladle, declared: "Soup puts the heart at ease, calms down the violence of hunger, eliminates the tensions of the day and refines the appetite." He might have added "and stretches the budget." But he didn't, so we will.

❀ *Autumn Chicken-Vegetable Soup*

1 broiler-fryer, cut up (2½ to 3 lbs.)

2 quarts water

salt

2 (8 oz.) cans or 1 (15 oz.) can tomato sauce with tomato bits

6 tiny whole white onions, peeled, or 2 medium onions, peeled and quartered

6 small carrots, pared

3 small stalks celery with tops, sliced diagonally

½ cup chopped fresh parsley

1 bay leaf

1 (8 oz.) can whole kernel corn, drained

Place chicken in kettle with tight-fitting cover; add water and 1 tablespoon salt. Simmer, covered, 1½ hours or until tender. Remove chicken and skim fat from broth; stir in tomato sauce, onions, carrots, celery, parsley, and bay leaf. Cover; simmer 30 minutes more or until vegetables are tender. Meanwhile, remove skin and bones from chicken, leaving meat in large pieces; add to broth along with corn when vegetables are tender. Salt to taste; simmer 5 to 10 minutes more or until thoroughly heated. Remove bay leaf. Makes 6 servings.

❀ *Celery Soup*

1 cup water

1 teaspoon salt

few grains pepper

2 cups diced celery

2 cups water

¾ cup nonfat dry milk solids

2 tablespoons flour

1 teaspoon salt

3 tablespoons grated onion

Combine first 4 ingredients in a saucepan. Cook over moderate heat for about 10 minutes, until celery is just tender. Place the 2 cups of water in the top of a double boiler; add dry milk, flour, and salt. Beat with rotary beater until smooth. Add onion, celery, and the celery cooking water. Cook over moderately low heat, stirring constantly, until mixture is smooth and thickened. Makes 3 servings.

✿ *Chicken-Corn Chowder*

1 to 1½ pounds chicken pieces (legs, thighs, or breasts)
1 cup water
2 teaspoons salt
2 tablespoons chopped parsley
2 tablespoons chopped celery leaves
2 carrots, cubed

2 medium potatoes, cubed
2 ribs celery, sliced
2 (8 oz.) cans or 1 (15 oz.) can tomato sauce with tomato bits
1 (1 lb. 1 oz.) can cream-style corn
¼ to ½ teaspoon poultry seasoning

Place chicken in soup kettle with water, 1 teaspoon salt, parsley, and celery leaves; cover, simmer ½ hour. Remove bones if desired. Add carrots, potatoes, celery, and remaining 1 teaspoon salt; simmer 15 to 20 minutes longer, until chicken and vegetables are tender. Add tomato sauce, corn, and poultry seasoning; simmer, stirring, until chowder thickens slightly. Makes 5 to 6 servings.

✿ *Chicken-Dumpling Soup*

1 broiler-fryer, cut up (3 lbs.)
1½ quarts water
2 teaspoons salt
½ teaspoon pepper
1 bay leaf
3 carrots, pared and cut in 1-inch pieces
2 potatoes, pared and cut in eighths

1 (8 oz.) can tomato sauce
minced onion
1 (10 oz.) package frozen corn
2 cups biscuit mix
¾ cup milk
2 tablespoons finely chopped fresh parsley

Place chicken in kettle with tight-fitting lid; add water, salt, pepper, and bay leaf. Simmer, covered, 1 hour or until tender. Remove chicken; skim fat from broth. Stir carrots, potatoes, tomato sauce, and onion into broth; simmer, covered, 1 hour. Meanwhile, remove skin and bones from chicken, leaving meat in large pieces; add to broth along with corn. Combine biscuit mix and milk; drop by tablespoonfuls on soup. Sprinkle dumplings with parsley. Simmer, uncovered, 10 minutes; cover and cook 10 minutes more. Makes 6 servings.

❀ Chicken Gumbo

1 cup chopped celery
1 onion, chopped
1 green pepper, chopped
2 tablespoons salad oil
1 tablespoon flour
6 cups chicken broth or
   bouillon
1 bay leaf
¼ teaspoon thyme
2 tablespoons chopped
   parsley

dash hot-pepper sauce
1 (10 oz.) package frozen
   okra or 1 (1 lb.) can okra,
   drained
2 cups diced cooked
   chicken
1 (5 oz.) can shrimp,
   drained
cooked rice

In Dutch oven cook celery, onion, and green pepper in salad oil until soft. Stir in flour, then broth, bay leaf, thyme, parsley, and hot-pepper sauce. Cover and simmer for 30 minutes. Add okra, chicken, and shrimp; simmer 5 minutes. Serve in soup bowls with scoop of rice on top. Makes 6 servings.

❀ Cold Fresh-Tomato Cream Soup

boiling water
1 pound tomatoes
1 (10½ oz.) can condensed
   onion soup, undiluted

1 cup cream
thin slices of midget dill
   pickles

Pour boiling water over tomatoes; let stand 1 minute; drain. Cover with cold water; drain. Carefully peel skin; cut out stems. Blend tomatoes, covered, in blender, to make a puree. Measure 2 cups. Return 2 cups puree to blender. Add onion soup at low speed and blend, covered, until well combined. Add cream; blend again to combine. Refrigerate until very well chilled, about 2 hours. To serve, turn soup into chilled mugs. Top each serving with a few pickle slices. Makes 4 to 6 servings.

❈ Corn Chowder

⅓ cup finely diced salt pork
1 medium onion, sliced
3 cups coarsely diced peeled potatoes
1 teaspoon salt

⅛ teaspoon pepper
water
1 (17 oz.) can cream-style corn
2 cups milk

Fry salt pork in heavy saucepan over low heat until crisp and brown. Remove browned pieces and reserve. Add onion to fat in saucepan and cook until golden brown. Add potatoes, salt, and pepper. Add just enough water to cover potatoes. Cook over very low heat until potatoes are tender, about 20 minutes. Add corn and milk; heat but do not boil. Let stand at least 2 hours to ripen. At serving time reheat slowly. Top each serving with the pork pieces. Makes 4 servings.

❈ Fish Chowder

1 strip bacon
¼ cup sliced celery
1 tablespoon chopped onion
1½ cups diced raw potatoes
2 cups water
1 pound fish fillets, cut into 1-inch-wide strips
1 teaspoon salt

dash of pepper
⅛ teaspoon dried marjoram leaves
3 tablespoons flour (optional)
⅓ cup cold water (optional)
1 cup milk
1 cup light cream
chopped fresh parsley

In medium saucepan cook bacon over moderately low heat until crisp. Remove from heat. Crumble the bacon and set aside. Drain off fat. In same saucepan combine celery, onion, potatoes, and water. Place over moderate heat and bring to a boil. Reduce heat to low and simmer, uncovered, 15 minutes. Add fish, salt, pepper, and marjoram. Simmer, uncovered, 10 minutes longer, or until potatoes are tender. (If a thickened chowder is desired: stir 3 tablespoons flour into ⅓ cup cold water, blend well; add flour mixture to chowder, stirring constantly; bring to a boil over moderate heat and boil 1 minute, stirring constantly.) Reduce heat to low. Add milk and cream and heat to serving temperature, about 5 minutes. Serve sprinkled with chopped parsley. Makes 6 servings.

❀ *Fish Soup*

2 pounds firm-fleshed
   whitefish (cod, haddock,
   or halibut), cut in large
   chunks
2 teaspoons salt
2 onions, sliced
¼ cup salad oil
1 (6 oz.) can tomato paste

6 cups water
¼ teaspoon red pepper
¼ teaspoon pepper
1 cup finely chopped fresh
   parsley
⅓ cup dry white wine
slices of Italian bread
   (toasted, if desired)

Sprinkle fish with ½ teaspoon salt; let stand 1 hour. Meanwhile, brown onions lightly in salad oil; pour off fat. Stir in tomato paste, water, red pepper, 1½ teaspoons salt, pepper, parsley, and wine. Simmer 30 minutes. Add fish; simmer about 10 minutes more, or just until fish flakes easily with a fork. To serve, place a slice of bread in each soup bowl; ladle soup over it. Makes 6 servings.

❀ *French Country Soup*

2 pounds beef shanks
2 quarts water
2 (8 oz.) cans tomato sauce
2 beef bouillon cubes
2 teaspoons sugar
1 teaspoon salt
¼ teaspoon pepper

2 whole cloves
2 onions, thinly sliced
3 turnips, peeled and diced
1 cup elbow macaroni
1 (16 oz.) can cut green
   beans, drained

In Dutch oven or deep kettle combine beef with water, tomato sauce, bouillon cubes, sugar, salt, pepper, and cloves. Bring to boil; simmer, covered, 2 hours. Add onions, turnips, macaroni, and green beans; simmer, uncovered, 20 minutes. Makes 6 to 8 servings.

❀ Ham and Lentils Soup

1 fully cooked ham
  shank (2 lbs.)
1½ cups dried lentils
7 cups water
3 tablespoons butter or
  margarine
½ cup chopped celery
½ cup chopped leek
½ cup chopped onion

1 small clove garlic, crushed
1¾ teaspoons salt
¼ teaspoon dried thyme
  leaves
¼ teaspoon coarsely
  ground black pepper
1 cup sliced frankfurters
  (about 3)

Trim excess fat from ham shank. In large kettle combine ham shank
and lentils with 5 cups cold water; bring to boil. Reduce heat and
simmer, covered, 1 hour. Meanwhile, melt butter in medium skillet.
Add celery, leek, onion, and garlic; sauté 5 minutes. Add sautéed
vegetables, salt, thyme, pepper, and 2 cups water to ham shank and
lentils. Simmer, covered, until lentils are tender—about 30 minutes.
Remove ham from soup; cool. Then cut meat from bone and dice.
With potato masher, mash vegetables right in kettle; leave some
lentils whole. Add diced ham to soup, along with frankfurters; simmer, covered, 30 minutes longer. For a very thick soup, simmer
uncovered. Makes 8 1-cup servings.

❀ Ham-It-Up Soup

1 pound dried beans or
  lentils
2½ quarts water
2 ham hocks (or 1 meaty
  ham bone)
1 cup chopped celery
1 carrot, chopped

2 (8 oz.) cans or 1 (15 oz.)
  can tomato sauce with
  tomato bits
½ teaspoon salt
1 teaspoon Worcestershire
  sauce
½ teaspoon seasoned salt
¼ teaspoon pepper

In Dutch oven or kettle combine all ingredients. Bring to boil; simmer, covered, 2 hours, stirring occasionally. Remove skin and bone
from ham; skim off fat from broth. Return meat to soup. Makes 6
to 8 servings.

❀ *Hearty Lunch Soup*

3 tablespoons salad oil
1 onion, chopped
¼ cup chopped green
   pepper
¼ cup diced celery
3 cups chicken bouillon
1 (8 oz.) can tomato sauce
¼ cup raw regular rice

1 (8 oz.) can kidney beans,
   with liquid
1 tablespoon chopped
   parsley
½ teaspoon salt
dash pepper
3 to 4 frankfurters, sliced

Sauté onion, green pepper, and celery in oil. Add all other ingredients. Bring to boil; reduce heat and simmer, covered, 20 to 30 minutes. Makes 4 to 5 servings.

❀ *Lentil Soup*

1 pound dried lentils
2½ quarts water
2 ham hocks (or 1 leftover
   meaty ham bone)
1 onion, chopped
1 cup chopped celery

1 carrot, pared and
   chopped
1 teaspoon salt
½ teaspoon seasoned salt
¼ teaspoon pepper
1 bay leaf

In Dutch oven or kettle combine all ingredients. Bring to boil; simmer, covered, 2½ hours, stirring occasionally. Remove skin and bone from ham hocks; skim fat from broth. Return meat to soup. Makes 6 to 8 servings.

❀ *Make-a-Meal Soup*

1½ pounds boneless chuck
   or stewing meat
6 cups water
1 teaspoon salt
¼ teaspoon pepper
1 small clove garlic, minced
1 bay leaf

2 stalks celery, sliced
2 carrots, sliced
1 onion, chopped
¼ head cabbage, chopped
3 tablespoons rice
1 (15 oz.) can red beans,
   with liquid

Cut meat into large bite-size pieces. Place first 6 ingredients in large kettle. Bring to boil and skim off surface. Cover and simmer 1½ hours, or until meat is almost tender. Add remaining ingredients and simmer, covered, 30 minutes. Makes 4 to 6 servings.

❁ *Manhattan Clam Chowder*

1 medium onion, chopped
½ cup chopped green pepper
1 clove garlic, crushed
2 tablespoons salad oil
1 quart water
2 (8 oz.) cans or 1 (15 oz.) can tomato sauce with tomato bits

2 (8 oz.) cans chopped clams, with liquid
1 (14½ oz.) can whole new potatoes, drained and cubed
1 teaspoon salt
½ teaspoon thyme
1 bay leaf

In kettle or Dutch oven cook onion, green pepper, and garlic in salad oil until tender; add remaining ingredients and bring to boil. Cover and simmer 1 hour. Remove bay leaf. Makes 6 servings.

❁ *Minestrone*

½ cup dried pea beans
4 tablespoons salad oil
1 cup shredded cabbage
½ cup slivered green beans
½ cup slivered celery
1 clove garlic, mashed
2 medium onions, chopped
6 cups beef stock made from beef bones, or 6 bouillon cubes dissolved in 6 cups boiling water

1 cup canned tomatoes
⅛ teaspoon thyme
2 teaspoons salt
½ teaspoon pepper
½ cup elbow macaroni
grated Parmesan cheese

Soak beans at least 12 hours. Drain and cover with water. Cook 1 hour, until skins loosen. Drain. Heat oil in large, heavy saucepan over low heat. Add cabbage, green beans, celery, garlic, and onions. Cook slowly until vegetables are soft. Add stock or bouillon cubes dissolved in boiling water, tomatoes, pea beans, thyme, salt, and pepper. Cover and simmer over low heat 45 minutes. Add macaroni; cook 15 minutes longer. Serve in warm soup bowls and sprinkle each serving with cheese. Makes 6 servings.

❀ Mulligatawny

2 cups cooked chicken or
  turkey pieces
¼ cup chopped carrot
¼ cup chopped green
  pepper
2 green apples, chopped
5 cups chicken or turkey
  stock, or 5 chicken
  bouillon cubes dissolved
  in 5 cups boiling water

1 (8 oz.) can tomato sauce
1 teaspoon chopped parsley
2 teaspoons curry powder
pinch mace
1 teaspoon salt
pinch pepper

Combine all ingredients and simmer, covered, for 20 to 30 minutes.
Makes 4 to 6 servings.

❀ Onion Soup

2 medium sweet onions,
  thinly sliced
2 tablespoons butter or
  margarine
1 tablespoon flour
1 quart beef stock made
  from beef bones, or 4
  bouillon cubes dissolved
  in 4 cups boiling water

½ bay leaf
½ teaspoon brown sugar
¼ teaspoon pepper
dash garlic powder
1½ teaspoons
  Worcestershire sauce
butter or margarine
4 slices French bread
grated Romano cheese

Heat butter in heavy saucepan over low heat. Add onions and cook
until golden brown. Sprinkle with flour and blend thoroughly. Add
beef stock or bouillon, bay leaf, brown sugar, pepper, garlic powder, and Worcestershire. Cover and simmer over very low heat 1
hour. Butter bread slices on both sides; place in a skillet over low
heat; brown on both sides. Float a bread slice on top of each serving
and sprinkle with cheese. Makes 4 servings.

❀ Portuguese Bean Soup

1 pound dried red beans	2 bay leaves
3½ quarts water	½ teaspoon ground allspice
3 onions, sliced	2 (6 oz.) cans tomato paste
2 cloves garlic, minced	3 potatoes, peeled and
½ pound salt pork, cut into	diced
thick slices	

Bring beans and water to boil in large kettle; boil for 2 minutes. Remove from heat and let stand 1 hour. Then bring to boil again and simmer, covered, for 1½ hours, or until beans are tender. Add remaining ingredients; simmer, covered, for another hour. Makes 6 to 8 servings.

❀ Scotch Broth

1 tablespoon salad oil	1 cup sliced carrots
2 pounds lamb neck pieces	1 cup sliced fresh green
6 cups boiling water	beans
1 bay leaf	1 (16 oz.) can tomatoes
2½ teaspoons salt	1 clove garlic, minced
½ teaspoon pepper	¼ cup chopped fresh
½ cup pearl barley	parsley
½ cup sliced onion	
1 cup chopped celery stalks	
and leaves	

Heat oil in Dutch oven over moderately high heat; brown lamb lightly. Pour off excess fat. Add water, bay leaf, salt, and pepper. Cover and simmer over low heat 1½ hours. Cool and chill several hours or overnight. Discard fat. Add barley; cover, bring to boil, reduce heat, and cook ½ hour. Add onions, celery, carrots, beans, tomatoes, and garlic; cook 45 minutes longer. Remove meat from bones, cut into large pieces, and return to soup. Stir in parsley just before serving. Makes 4 to 5 servings.

✿ Seafood Chowder

1 cup chopped onion
½ cup chopped green
  pepper
1 clove garlic, crushed
2 tablespoons salad oil
3 (8 oz.) cans tomato sauce
¼ cup rice
2 (7 oz.) cans tuna, drained

1 (4 oz.) can shrimp,
  drained
1 teaspoon salt
1 bay leaf
¼ teaspoon thyme
dash cayenne
1 quart hot water

Sauté onion, green pepper, and garlic in salad oil. Add remaining ingredients and bring to boil. Cover and simmer 1 hour. Makes 4 servings.

✿ Spinach Soup

2 cups finely chopped raw
  spinach
⅔ cup diced carrot
6 scallions, chopped

6 cups chicken broth
½ teaspoon salt
pepper
grated Parmesan cheese

Place first 6 ingredients in saucepan; bring to boil and cook over moderate heat 30 minutes, stirring occasionally. If desired, serve with grated Parmesan cheese. Makes 4 to 6 servings.

✿ Super Soup Bowl

1½ pounds boneless lean
  beef brisket, chuck, or
  stewing meat, cut in large
  bite-size pieces
4 cups water
1 teaspoon salt
¼ teaspoon pepper
1 small clove garlic, minced
1 small bay leaf
2 stalks celery, sliced
  (about 1 cup)

2 medium carrots, sliced
  (about ¾ cup)
1 small onion, cut in wedges
¼ small head cabbage, cut
  in 1-inch wedges
3 tablespoons pearl barley
  or rice
2 (8 oz.) cans tomato sauce
1 (15½ oz.) can red or
  kidney beans, with liquid

Place meat, water, salt, and pepper in large kettle or Dutch oven.

Slowly bring to boil; skim. Add garlic and bay leaf. Reduce heat, cover, and simmer 1½ hours, or until meat is almost tender; remove bay leaf. Add fresh vegetables, barley, and tomato sauce. Simmer, covered, 20 minutes. Add beans. Simmer, covered, 10 minutes more, or until vegetables are tender. Makes 4 servings.

❀ *Turkey Noodle Soup*

1 turkey carcass, cut in
   small pieces
water
1 cup sliced celery

1 onion, sliced
1 cup sliced carrots
salt to taste
8 ounces medium noodles

Place cut-up turkey carcass in large kettle and cover with water. Cover kettle and simmer 1½ hours. Skim surface to remove excess fat. Add vegetables, tomato sauce, and salt. Simmer 15 minutes. Add noodles and simmer 15 more minutes. Makes 4 to 6 servings.

❀ *Vegetable Soup*

1 pound stewing meat, cut
   in 1-inch pieces
2 tablespoons salad oil
4 cups water
1 onion, chopped

1 cup sliced carrots
1 cup chopped celery
1 (14½ oz.) can whole
   tomatoes
1 tablespoon seasoned salt

Brown meat in salad oil in large pot. Add water; simmer, covered, 1½ hours. Add vegetables, tomatoes, and salt. Cook 30 to 40 minutes longer, or until vegetables are tender. Makes 4 servings.

❀ *Vegetable-Beef Soup*

1 to 1½ pounds beef shank
   bone with meat
1½ quarts water
2 bay leaves
3 sprigs parsley
1 tablespoon salt

1 cup diced carrots
1 cup diced potatoes
1 cup sliced celery
¼ cup rice
1 quart water

Put first 5 ingredients in large kettle. Cover and simmer until meat is tender, about 2½ hours. Skim broth. Cut meat from bone; return to broth. Add remaining ingredients; cover and simmer about 25 minutes. Makes 4 to 6 servings.

❀ *Watercress and Potato Soup*

1 *quart chicken broth*   *salt and pepper*
2 *medium potatoes, diced*   1 *cup hot milk*
1 *cup coarsely chopped*
  watercress

Heat broth over moderately low heat; add potatoes and watercress. Cover and cook about 45 minutes, or until tender. Mash through a strainer or a food mill. Season with salt and pepper. Add milk; heat and serve. Makes 5 servings.

BEEF, LAMB, AND VEAL

Meats are the major item in any food budget. A recent statistic says that Americans are eating more meat than ever—each of us consumes 183 pounds of meat annually, 110 pounds of which is beef. Obviously, if the homemaker can keep a firm hold on meat spending, she will have much more control over her total grocery expenses.

Unfortunately, most of us think of meat in terms of juicy steaks and prime ribs, which bear the highest price tags. We must learn how to shop for the less familiar, less expensive cuts of meat, which are every bit as nutritious as their more costly counterparts. If you are not well acquainted with the various cuts of meat, get a meat manual with meat charts at your local library and do a little homework before you head for the butcher's.

In shopping for meat, always take advantage of special sales. Stock up and keep those "buys" in your freezer. Buy meats listed as "plentiful" by the U. S. Department of Agriculture. Shop for advertised specials and buy larger cuts.

Chuck roast is a good example of how buying a larger cut can mean larger savings. A 9-pound blade chuck roast, 4½ inches thick, yields enough high protein, boneless meat for three meals at a minimum cost for each dinner. It will give you a 3- to 3½-pound pot roast from the center piece; four boneless steaks about 8 ounces each from the smaller rib muscle; and 2 pounds of meat for stew, soup, or casserole by boning off the meat around the flat blade bone.

Beef brisket is a favorite beef cut of thrifty shoppers. That's because a well trimmed beef brisket has little fat and a wealth of juices. One 4- to 5-pound brisket can provide enough meat for two meals, plus sliced meat for sandwiches.

If you want to slim down your meat expenses, explore the subject of bones with your butcher—you'll be amazed at what you discover. Beef bones, marrow bones, ox tails, neck bones, can be turned into very economical but satisfying meals. Neck bones, for example, may have a lot of fat and bone waste, but the cost per pound is low. Buy at least ¾ to 1 pound of bones per serving. You'll find the little pieces of beef from neck bones especially succulent and good in casseroles, sandwich fillings, main dish salads—almost any recipe that calls for slivers of cooked meat.

Like "Smith" or "Jones" in a telephone directory, the name "chuck" pops up most often at the meat counter. It's easy to get confused about which chuck is which. Actually, beef chuck answers to a score of titles including center cut, blade, 7-bone, shoulder, cross-arm, and round bone. Each gets its name from the location in the chuck of the animal, and each makes a great pot roast. When in doubt about chuck cuts, ask your meat man. He will be happy to help you. Just don't expect him to hold a long conversation with you at busy times in the store; pick a slow time to ask your questions.

We read somewhere that a survey on eating habits indicated that people who enjoy lamb are intelligent and/or mature. Since a leg of spring lamb can rival a porterhouse steak in price, it might also be said that they are financially secure. At any rate, lamb is a delightful treat and its so-called intelligent consumers know that the best lamb is pinkish-red in color, fine-grained and smooth, with firm, brittle, and flaky fat, either pinkish or white.

"Spring" lamb comes from animals born in the fall and held to spring for slaughtering. "Genuine" spring lamb comes from animals just a few months old and is available from March through May. More tender but actually less flavorful than spring lamb, it is also more expensive. "Old" lamb, of course, becomes mutton—and turns up most often as chops or stew meat.

One way to have your lamb and your money, too, is to buy lamb patties. Patties are usually equal in price to ground chuck. Otherwise, watch for lamb when it's on the "plentiful" list for best prices.

Veal is acclaimed as the gourmet's meat. Veal, actually the meat of young beef, is mild in flavor, low in fat, and grayish-pink in color. Its delicate flavor resembles chicken, and the two are interchangeable in many recipes. Veal combines well with other foods, and its taste can be enhanced also by the use of flavorful sauces. Since the meat has so little fat, veal requires somewhat longer and slower cooking than beef or lamb to make it tender. Veal roasts and steaks, for example, lack fat and have a good amount of connective tissue; they are best when cooked slowly for a long time. There is one form of veal—the veal scallop—that does call for quick cooking. A veal scallop is a small boneless cut, usually from the leg, which is pounded very thin. If your market does not have veal scallops, you may make them yourself by pounding a veal cutlet with a mallet until the meat is very thin, and then cutting the meat into round or oval pieces about four inches in diameter.

Again, if you are interested in saving money on veal purchases, buy specials or when the meat is put in the "plentiful" class. Ground veal alone lacks character but is excellent combined with ground beef in meat loaf or patties.

Since all meat shrinks in cooking, plan on ¼ to ½ pound of meat without bone for individual servings. Double this estimate for cuts that include the bone. Using a steady, low temperature in cooking will help keep down meat shrinkage.

One last thought on the subject of meat shopping: put meat at the top of your marketing list. Decorators advise their clients to choose the rug first, then the wallpaper, drapes, and furniture to go with it. Fashion experts always emphasize that one should buy the dress first, not the shoes, gloves, or other accessories. So it is when you're shopping for the day's or week's meals. Buy the meat first, then you'll know what vegetable and dessert "accessories" will best accompany the main dish.

Cost-Per-Serving Chart

To get the most value from the meat you buy, you must compare the actual amount of lean (the protein part) to the amount of waste (bone, fat, and gristle) in each pound. Learn to judge value by the cost per serving of the meat you buy rather than the cost per pound. Figuring cost per serving is not as difficult as it sounds.

Here is a handy guide to help you figure the number of servings you can plan on from the meats you usually buy.

For meat with no bone or fat

Allow 4 to 5 servings per pound

For meat with little bone or fat

Allow 3 to 4 servings per pound

For meat with medium bone or fat
    Allow 2 to 3 servings per pound
For meat with a large amount of bone or fat
    Allow 1 to 2 servings per pound
    The more detailed chart following will let you quickly figure the cost per serving of many cuts of meat. An average price range of cost per pound is listed across the top, and the number of servings per pound appears at the left. Put your finger on the price per pound and move it down that column of figures until parallel with the cut of meat you are buying. The cost per serving will be the figure directly below the price per pound.

	Price Per Pound	.29	.39	.49	.59	.69	.79	.89	.99	1.09	1.19	1.29	1.39
	Beef Chuck blade steak Chuck arm steak Chuck roast—blade												
	Cost Per Serving												
SERVING TWO	Chuck roast— arm	.15	.20	.25	.30	.35	.40	.45	.50	.55	.60	.65	.70
	Pork Picnic (bone in) Ham steaks												
	Poultry Broiler (ready to cook)												
	Beef Chuck roast (boneless) Brisket Round Sirloin tip												
SERVING THREE	Pork Blade steaks Ham (bone in) Boston butt (bone in) Ribs, farm or country style	.10	.13	.16	.20	.23	.26	.30	.33	.36	.40	.43	.46
	Poultry Legs, thighs												

		.07	.10	.12	.15	.17	.20	.22	.25	.27	.30	.32	.35
	Beef Ground beef												
	Pork Center cut or rib chops												
SERVING FOUR	Sausage												
	Ham (boneless and canned)												
	Poultry Breasts												
	Fish Fillets, steaks, sticks												

❀ Barbecued Steak

1 package instant meat
  marinade
⅓ cup water
⅓ cup red wine
1 clove garlic, crushed

1 tablespoon chili sauce
½ teaspoon dried basil
  leaves
2¾ pound beef chuck
  steak, cut 1½ inches thick

Blend meat marinade, water, and wine together; stir in garlic, chili sauce, and basil. Pour over meat in a shallow pan. Pierce all surfaces of meat thoroughly with a fork. Marinate only 15 minutes, turning and piercing with a fork frequently. Remove meat and reserve marinade. Place steak on broiler rack in preheated broiler 3 to 4 inches from heat and broil 15 minutes, brushing occasionally with the marinade. Turn and broil 10 minutes more, or until cooked to the desired degree of doneness, brushing occasionally with marinade. Makes 5 to 6 servings.

❀ Bavarian Pot Roast

3 pounds lean, boneless
  chuck roast
¼ cup flour
1½ teaspoons salt
1 teaspoon ground ginger
½ teaspoon ground allspice
½ teaspoon ground cloves
¼ teaspoon pepper
3 tablespoons salad oil

1 (8 oz.) can tomato sauce
  with mushrooms
¾ cup water
½ cup red wine
¼ cup cider vinegar
2 onions, sliced
2 tablespoons sugar
1 bay leaf

Coat roast with flour mixed with seasonings. Brown well on both sides in salad oil in Dutch oven; remove excess fat. Add remaining ingredients. Cover; simmer 2½ hours, or until tender. Remove roast to a platter and thicken liquid for gravy. Makes 6 to 8 servings.

❀ Beef and Kidney Pie

1 pound beef chuck steak
½ pound lamb kidneys
¼ cup flour
½ teaspoon salt
⅛ teaspoon pepper
4 tablespoons beef fat
    drippings or other fat

1 cup chopped onion
1 bay leaf
2 tablespoons chopped
    celery leaves
2 cups water
1 cup thinly sliced carrots
1 recipe plain pastry

Cut steak into 1-inch cubes. Remove tough membrane from kidneys and cut each into about 4 pieces. Combine flour, salt, and pepper; sprinkle over meats. Heat fat in large heavy skillet over moderate heat. Add meats and brown well. Remove meats; add onion to skillet and brown lightly. Return meats; add bay leaf, celery, and water. Cover tightly and simmer over low heat 1 hour. Add carrots. Heat oven to 425°. Roll out half the pastry on a lightly floured board and line a shallow 1½-quart casserole with it. Pour in meat mixture. Roll out rest of pastry to fit top. Make crosswise slits in center and fold back corners. Place pastry on top of casserole; seal and flute the edge like a pie. Bake 30 minutes, until pastry is brown. Makes 4 to 6 servings.

❀ Beef Roulades

2 pounds round steak,
    thinly sliced
6 slices bacon
2 tablespoons salad oil
1 small onion, chopped
1 cup beef consommé
½ teaspoon salt

2 (8 oz.) cans tomato sauce
    with mushrooms
2 tablespoons minced
    parsley
½ teaspoon thyme
buttered noodles or rice

Cut meat the length and width of a slice of bacon. Lay 1 bacon slice on each strip of meat, roll up tight, and tie with string. Brown on all sides in hot oil. Remove roulades from pan and place in shallow baking dish. Brown onion lightly in skillet; stir in consommé, salt, tomato sauce, parsley, and thyme. Pour over meat. Cover; bake at 375° for 1 hour. Remove cover and bake an additional hour. Serve with noodles or rice. Makes 6 to 8 servings.

🏵 Boiled Beef Brisket

4 pounds brisket of beef	*12 whole black peppers*
2½ quarts water	*1 bay leaf*
2 leeks, cut up	*2 teaspoons salt*
2 carrots, pared, quartered	*1 teaspoon dried thyme*
2 stalks celery, coarsely cut	*leaves*

Bring 2½ quarts water to boil in large kettle. Trim excess fat from beef. To water, add beef and other ingredients. Bring to boil. Then reduce heat; simmer, covered, about 3½ hours, until tender. Remove meat to heated platter. Makes 8 servings. Good served with horseradish sauce.

🏵 Braised Beef with Cabbage

2 tablespoons salad oil	*1 teaspoon sugar*
1 pound beef chuck, cut into 1½-inch cubes	*1 teaspoon salt*
	⅛ teaspoon pepper
2 onions, thinly sliced	*1 (2 lb.) head green cabbage*
1 cup water	
1 apple, pared, cored, and thinly sliced	*4 potatoes, pared and quartered lengthwise*
1 (1 lb.) can tomatoes, with liquid	

Heat oil in large skillet. Add beef and brown on all sides. Remove. Add onions to skillet and cook slowly until golden brown. Add browned beef; stir in 1 cup water. Add apple and tomatoes. Sprinkle with sugar, salt, and pepper. Bring to boil; reduce heat and simmer, covered, 2 hours. Trim outer leaves, if damaged, from cabbage. Cut cabbage into quarters and cook in rapidly boiling salted water 5 minutes. Drain. Add potatoes and cabbage to meat mixture; simmer, covered, 1 hour longer. Makes 4 servings.

🌼 Braised Stuffed Flank Steak

1 flank steak, scored (about 2 lbs.)
1 teaspoon Worcestershire sauce
1 teaspoon salt
¼ cup butter or margarine
2 tablespoons chopped onion
1 cup soft bread crumbs
¼ teaspoon salt
⅛ teaspoon paprika
3 tablespoons chopped celery
1 egg, slightly beaten
flour
2 tablespoons soft shortening
1 beef bouillon cube
1 cup boiling water
1 tablespoon flour
1 cup tomato juice
¼ teaspoon salt

Brush inside of flank steak with Worcestershire sauce. Sprinkle with 1 teaspoon salt. Melt butter in a skillet, add onion, and cook until tender. Add bread crumbs, ¼ teaspoon salt, paprika, celery, and egg. Combine thoroughly. Spread dressing over inside of steak. Roll loosely; fasten with skewers and lace skewers securely with string. Dust rolled meat with flour. Heat shortening in a large saucepan or Dutch oven over moderate heat. Brown roll thoroughly, turning to brown all sides. Heat oven to 350°. Dissolve bouillon cube in boiling water. Gradually add ¼ cup of bouillon mixture to the 1 tablespoon flour. Stir in remainder of beef bouillon, tomato juice, and ¼ teaspoon salt. Pour over steak roll. Cover tightly; bake 1½ to 2 hours, or until fork tender. Place roll on serving platter; remove skewers and string. Skim excess fat from gravy in pan and serve gravy with sliced meat. Makes 6 to 8 servings.

🌼 Braised Swiss Steak

1½ pounds round steak, 1½ inches thick
3 tablespoons flour
2 tablespoons salad oil
½ cup chopped onion
½ cup grated carrot
2 tablespoons chopped parsley
3 whole cloves
2 bay leaves
1 teaspoon salt
½ teaspoon liquid gravy seasoning
¼ teaspoon dried thyme leaves
⅛ teaspoon pepper
1¼ cups water

Wipe steak with damp paper towels. Coat with 2 tablespoons flour.

In hot oil in large skillet, brown steak well on both sides—15 to 20 minutes in all. Add onion, carrot, parsley, cloves, bay leaves, salt, gravy seasoning, thyme, pepper, and 1 cup water; bring to boil. Reduce heat and simmer, covered, 2 to 2½ hours, or until steak is fork tender. Remove steak to serving platter. Combine remaining 1 tablespoon flour with ¼ cup water. Stir into liquid in skillet; bring to boil. Reduce heat and simmer 3 minutes. Spoon some gravy over steak and pass the rest. Makes 4 servings.

❀ Broiled Western Steak

1 chuck steak, 1 inch thick   *½ teaspoon salt*
(about 3½ lbs.)   *¼ teaspoon pepper*
instant meat tenderizer   *⅛ teaspoon garlic powder*
¼ cup margarine, softened
1 tablespoon chopped
parsley

Wipe steak with damp paper towels. Sprinkle with instant meat tenderizer as package label directs. Place on rack in broiler and broil 3 to 4 inches from heat, about 10 minutes per side for medium rare. Meanwhile, in small bowl cream margarine with parsley, salt, pepper, and garlic powder. Place steak on hot serving platter; spread with seasoned margarine. Cut on the diagonal into slices about ½ inch thick. Serve at once. Makes 6 to 8 servings.

❀ Carbonade Beef Stew

⅓ cup flour   *1 clove garlic, crushed*
1½ teaspoons salt   *1 tablespoon chopped*
pepper   *parsley*
1¾ pounds beef, cut into   *⅛ teaspoon dried thyme*
1½-inch cubes   *leaves*
¼ cup salad oil   *1 bay leaf*
3 cups thinly sliced onions   *1½ teaspoons salt*
1 cup beer   *⅛ teaspoon pepper*

Place flour, 1½ teaspoons salt, and few grains of pepper in plastic or paper bag. Shake meat, a few pieces at a time, in bag until coated with flour mixture. Heat oil in Dutch oven or heavy saucepan; add beef cubes and cook over moderate heat until lightly browned. Remove meat; add onions and cook until tender. Return meat to pot;

add beer, garlic, parsley, thyme, bay leaf, 1½ teaspoons salt, and
⅛ teaspoon pepper. Cover and simmer 2½ to 3 hours, or until fork
tender. Makes 4 servings.

✤ Chinese Beef

1½ to 2 pounds flank steak   *few grains pepper*
1 tablespoon salad oil   *½ cup thinly sliced celery*
½ cup coarsely chopped   *1 small green pepper, sliced*
* onion*   *1 (16 oz.) can bean sprouts,*
1½ cups diluted beef broth   * drained*
2 tablespoons soy sauce   *1 tablespoon cornstarch*
½ teaspoon ground ginger   *1 tablespoon water*
1 cup thinly sliced carrots

Slice steak thinly and remove as much fat as possible. Heat oil in
large skillet over moderately high heat; add sliced steak a few
pieces at a time and cook until slices are browned. Remove beef
and reduce heat to moderately low. Add onion and cook until tender, stirring occasionally. Return meat to skillet and add beef broth,
soy sauce, ginger, carrots, and pepper; cover and cook 5 minutes.
Uncover and add celery, green pepper, and bean sprouts; cover and
cook 5 minutes. Mix cornstarch and water together. Stir into beef
mixture and cook 4 to 5 minutes, until thickened. Makes 6 to 8
servings.

✤ Company Beef and Peaches

2 to 3 pounds boneless   *2 tablespoons brown sugar*
* bottom or eye of round*   *2 tablespoons lemon juice*
* roast*   *1 tablespoon prepared*
2 tablespoons salad oil   * mustard*
salt   *1 teaspoon Worcestershire*
pepper   * sauce*
1 (8 oz.) can sliced peaches   *1 clove garlic, crushed*
* in syrup*   *2 tablespoons cold water*
1 (8 oz.) can tomato sauce   *1 tablespoon cornstarch*
* with onions*

Cut meat across the grain in 1-inch slices. In large skillet brown meat
in salad oil on both sides; sprinkle with salt and pepper. Move meat
to one side of skillet. Into skillet drain syrup from peaches; reserve

peaches. Stir in tomato sauce, brown sugar, lemon juice, mustard, Worcestershire, and garlic; turn meat in sauce until well coated. Simmer, covered, 1½ to 2 hours, or until meat is fork tender, turning meat occasionally. Remove meat to heated serving platter and keep warm. Blend water and cornstarch until smooth; add to drippings; bring to boil and cook until smooth and slightly thickened. Add peaches and heat thoroughly. Serve sauce and peaches with meat. Makes 6 to 8 servings.

❀ *Creole Liver*

2 (8 oz.) cans or 1 (15 oz.)
   can tomato sauce with
   tomato bits
½ cup chopped green
   pepper
½ cup chopped celery
½ cup chopped onion

⅓ cup water
salt
pepper
3 slices bacon, diced
1 pound baby beef or calf
   liver, thinly sliced

In saucepan simmer tomato sauce, green pepper, celery, onion, water, and ¼ teaspoon salt 15 minutes. Meanwhile, in skillet cook bacon until crisp; remove bits from skillet and add to simmering sauce. Cook liver quickly on both sides in bacon drippings; do not overcook (allow about 3 minutes per side). Pour off fat. Sprinkle lightly with salt and pepper. Pour sauce over liver; simmer 2 to 3 minutes. Makes 4 servings.

❀ *Dilly Beef with Sour Cream*

⅓ cup flour
1 teaspoon salt
¼ teaspoon pepper
1¾ pounds beef, cut into 1-
   inch cubes
3 tablespoons shortening
1½ cups hot water
1 clove garlic, crushed

1 bay leaf
¾ teaspoon dill seed
½ teaspoon salt
2 teaspoons paprika
¾ cup commercial sour
   cream
1 tablespoon flour

Place ⅓ cup flour, 1 teaspoon salt, and the pepper in a plastic or paper bag. Shake meat a few pieces at a time in the bag until coated with flour mixture. Melt shortening in Dutch oven or heavy saucepan; add beef cubes and cook over moderate heat until lightly browned. Add water, garlic, bay leaf, dill, and ½ teaspoon salt. Cover and cook over low heat 2½ to 3 hours, or until fork tender, adding water if necessary to maintain about ½ inch liquid in the pot. Sprinkle with paprika and simmer 5 minutes. Remove from heat. Mix sour cream and 1 tablespoon flour together; stir in ½ cup of the meat juices. Gradually stir sour cream mixture into juices in pot; cook over low heat until slightly thickened, stirring constantly. If desired, serve with noodles or rice. Makes 6 servings.

✿ Dilly Roast

1 7-bone chuck roast (3 to 4 lbs.)
2 tablespoons salad oil
½ teaspoon salt
⅛ teaspoon pepper
2 (8 oz.) cans tomato sauce with onion
1 cup water
2 tablespoons dill pickle juice
2 tablespoons cornstarch
⅓ cup chopped dill pickles

In electric skillet heated to 375° or in regular skillet over medium heat, brown meat in salad oil on both sides. Sprinkle with salt and pepper. Reduce heat, add 1 can tomato sauce, water, and dill pickle juice. Simmer, covered, 2 hours, or until meat is fork tender. Remove meat to platter and keep warm. Skim fat from drippings. Blend cornstarch with second can of tomato sauce; stir into drippings. Bring to boil, then cook, stirring, until smooth and thickened. Stir in dill pickles. Slice roast and spoon sauce over. Makes 6 to 8 servings.

✿ Easy Five-Hour Stew

2 pounds lean stewing beef, cut in small cubes
12 small white boiling onions
1 cup chopped celery
2 potatoes, cut in eighths
6 carrots, cut in 1-inch pieces
1 slice white bread, cubed
2 (8 oz.) cans tomato sauce
1 cup water
1½ teaspoons salt
⅛ teaspoon pepper

Combine all ingredients in casserole; cover and bake at 250° for 5 hours. Makes 6 to 8 servings.

❈ *Family Chuck Grill*

2 pounds chuck steak, cut   1 tablespoon salad oil
   ½ to ¾ inch thick   1 tablespoon horseradish
1 (8 oz.) can tomato sauce   1 teaspoon sugar
1 small onion, thinly sliced   ½ teaspoon salt
⅓ cup vinegar   ⅛ teaspoon pepper

Trim fat from meat and pierce both sides with fork; place in shallow dish (not metal). Combine remaining ingredients; pour over meat. Refrigerate, covered, several hours. Drain steak, reserving marinade. Broil steak or grill over glowing charcoal 4 to 5 inches from source of heat. Allow 20 to 25 minutes total cooking time for medium. Turn steak only once. While steak grills, simmer remaining marinade about 3 minutes; serve over steak. Makes 4 servings.

❈ *Fruited Pot Roast*

3 tablespoons flour   ⅛ teaspoon pepper
½ teaspoon salt   ½ pound pitted dried
⅛ teaspoon pepper   prunes
4 to 4¾ pounds pot roast   8 to 10 small white onions
2 tablespoons shortening   5 small carrots, cut into
1 cup dry white wine   halves
1 medium onion, sliced   ½ cup dry white wine
1 clove garlic, chopped   ½ cup water
1 bay leaf   3 tablespoons flour
pinch dried thyme leaves   ½ teaspoon salt
1 teaspoon salt

Mix 3 tablespoons flour, ½ teaspoon salt, and ⅛ teaspoon pepper; coat meat with mixture. Melt shortening in Dutch oven or heavy saucepan; add meat and cook over moderate heat until lightly browned on all sides. Remove meat from pot and drain off fat. Return meat to pot and add 1 cup wine, sliced onion, garlic, bay leaf, thyme, 1 teaspoon salt, and ⅛ teaspoon pepper. Cover and simmer 2¾ hours; if necessary, add water during cooking to maintain about 1 inch of liquid in the pot. Add prunes, onions, carrots, and the remaining ½ cup wine; continue cooking 45 minutes, or until vegetables and meat are fork tender, adding a little water if necessary. Remove meat, prunes, and vegetables to warm platter. Pour meat juices into a quart measuring cup and skim off fat. If necessary, add water to meat juices to make 2 cups; pour back into pot. Pour ½ cup water into a jar or gravy maker; add 3 tablespoons flour and ½ teaspoon salt; shake until blended. Pour into meat juices and cook and stir over low heat until thickened. Serve with pot roast. Makes 8 servings.

❀ *Home-Style Steak*

2 pounds round steak
1 (8 oz.) can tomato sauce
  with mushrooms
¾ cup chopped onion
½ cup chopped green
  pepper

2 tablespoons salad oil
1 teaspoon salt
1 teaspoon prepared
  mustard
¼ teaspoon pepper

Place meat on large sheet of heavy-duty aluminum foil. Combine remaining ingredients and pour over meat. Bring ends of foil up over meat and wrap tightly; seal securely so none of marinade can leak out. Place foil package in baking pan and refrigerate 2 hours or overnight. Bake at 350° for 1½ to 2 hours, or until meat is fork tender. Open foil to test meat, being careful not to puncture foil. Arrange meat on heated platter; pour some of sauce over meat and pass the rest in heated sauce boat. Makes 6 servings.

❀ *Individual Pot Roasts*

3 pounds boneless beef pot
  roast
salt
pepper
¼ cup salad oil
1 clove garlic, minced
1 cup sliced celery
2 (8 oz.) cans tomato sauce
1½ cups water
2 teaspoons salt

¼ teaspoon pepper
6 small potatoes, peeled
  and halved
6 small white onions
6 carrots, cut in half
1 (10 oz.) package frozen
  green beans
¼ cup flour
¼ cup water

Cut beef into 6 uniform pieces. Sprinkle with salt and pepper. Brown well in salad oil with garlic in Dutch oven. Add celery, tomato sauce, water, 2 teaspoons salt, and ¼ teaspoon pepper. Cover and simmer 2 hours, or until meat is tender. Add vegetables and cook 20 to 25 minutes longer. Remove meat to platter and keep warm. To make gravy, mix flour with ¼ cup water; add this mixture to liquid in Dutch oven. Simmer until thickened. Makes 6 servings.

❀ *Kidney Stew and Rice*

1 pound beef kidney	3 cups water
1 onion, chopped	1 (8 oz.) can tomato sauce
3 tablespoons salad oil	2 cups sliced carrots
2 teaspoons salt	2 stalks celery, sliced
½ teaspoon pepper	1 teaspoon salt
1 bay leaf	hot cooked rice
1 tablespoon Worcestershire sauce	

Remove skin, fat, and white veins from kidney. Cut in ¼-inch slices, then in pieces. Cover with cold water, drain, and dry. Cook kidney with onion in salad oil. Add seasonings, water, and tomato sauce. Bring to boil, cover, and simmer 1 hour. Add vegetables and salt; simmer 30 minutes longer. Serve with hot rice. Makes 4 servings.

❀ *Oxtail Stew*

2 tablespoons soft shortening	1½ teaspoons salt
2 pounds oxtail, cut into about 2-inch lengths	¼ teaspoon pepper
flour	4 medium onions, peeled and halved
2 cups hot water	4 medium potatoes, peeled and halved
1 medium-size onion, sliced	4 carrots, peeled and halved crosswise
1 (1 lb.) can tomatoes	
1 can beef consommé	

Heat shortening in large saucepan or Dutch oven over moderate heat. Roll meat pieces in flour to coat lightly. Brown meat well on all sides. Add hot water, onion, tomatoes, undiluted consommé, salt, and pepper. Cover and simmer 2½ hours, or until meat is fork tender. Add vegetables; simmer, covered, about 20 minutes until vegetables are tender. Skim off excess fat before serving. Makes 4 to 6 servings.

❀ Polynesian Beef

2¾ pounds beef chuck
  steak, cut about 1½
  inches thick
3 tablespoons salad oil
½ cup water
¼ cup soy sauce
½ teaspoon sugar
⅛ teaspoon pepper
3 medium tomatoes, cut
  into wedges

3 scallions, cut into ½-inch
  slices
1 medium green pepper,
  cut into strips
1 (5 oz.) can water chestnuts, drained and sliced
cooked rice

Slice steak thinly and cut into pieces about 3 inches long and ¾ inch
wide. Melt oil in large skillet and brown meat slices over moderate
heat. Mix water, soy sauce, sugar, and pepper; pour over meat.
Cover and simmer over low heat 1½ hours, or until fork tender. Add
tomatoes, scallions, green pepper, and water chestnuts; simmer 15
minutes longer. Serve with hot cooked rice. Makes 6 servings.

❀ Puchero à la Madrilena

½ pound lean beef, cubed
1 pound chicken, cut into
  serving-size pieces
salt
pepper
1 tablespoon salad oil
1½ tablespoons tomato
  sauce
2 medium onions, chopped
2 cloves garlic, minced

1 cup canned chick peas
  (liquid drained and
  reserved)
4 small potatoes, peeled
2 cups canned tomatoes
1 pound cabbage, cored
  and cut into wedges
2 teaspoons salt
⅛ teaspoon pepper

Sprinkle beef and chicken with salt and pepper. Heat oil in skillet
over moderately high heat; add beef and chicken and brown on all
sides. Remove meat and add tomato sauce; add onions and garlic
and cook until tender. Return meat to pan; add chick peas (reserving liquid), potatoes, tomatoes, cabbage, salt, and pepper. Add

some of the liquid from the chick peas and enough boiling water to cover meat and vegetables. Cook, covered, over low heat 1½ to 2 hours, or until meat is tender. Makes 4 to 5 servings.

✿ Quick Sauerbraten

3 *tablespoons flour*	1 *bay leaf*
1 *teaspoon salt*	½ *teaspoon each of ground*
⅛ *teaspoon pepper*	*allspice, cloves, and*
4 *to 4¾ pounds pot roast*	*cinnamon*
3 *tablespoons shortening*	½ *cup seedless raisins*
½ *cup water*	2 *tablespoons flour*
½ *cup cider vinegar*	¼ *cup gingersnap cookie*
1 *cup thinly sliced onion*	*crumbs*
1 *slice lemon*	

Mix 3 tablespoons flour, salt, and pepper; coat meat with mixture. Melt shortening in Dutch oven or heavy saucepan; add meat and cook over moderate heat until lightly browned on all sides. Remove meat from pot and drain off fat. Add water, vinegar, onion, lemon, bay leaf, allspice, cloves, and cinnamon; mix well. Return meat to pot; cover and simmer 2¾ hours. Add raisins and cook ½ hour longer, until meat is fork tender. Remove meat to warm platter. Pour meat juices into quart measuring cup; skim off fat. Add water if necessary to make 2½ cups liquid. Pour 2 tablespoons of the fat back into pot and blend in 2 tablespoons flour. Gradually add meat juices. Stir in gingersnap crumbs. Cook over moderate heat until thickened. Serve gravy with meat. Makes 8 servings.

✿ Roast Beef au Poivre

6 *pounds sirloin tip beef*	*salt*
roast or eye of round,	*baking potatoes*
rolled and tied	2 *tablespoons flour*
¼ *cup coarsely cracked*	1 *teaspoon salt*
black pepper	1½ *cups water*

Preheat oven to 325°. Wipe roast with damp paper towels. Roll roast in black pepper to coat surface completely; sprinkle with salt. Place on rack in shallow roasting pan. Insert meat thermometer into thickest part of roast. Roast, uncovered, 3 hours, or until meat thermometer registers 140°. (For tenderness, this cut of meat should be cooked only to rare.) After beef has roasted 1 hour, place potatoes around roast. When done, arrange roast and potatoes on serving platter. Keep warm. Pour drippings into measuring cup; carefully spoon off excess fat and discard. Return drippings to roasting pan. Stir in flour and 1 teaspoon salt, stirring to loosen browned bits in pan. Gradually stir in 1½ cups water. Bring to boil, stirring constantly. Reduce heat and simmer 5 minutes. Strain. Carve roast, slicing very thinly on the diagonal. Pass gravy. Makes 12 servings.

❀ Roast in Foil

It's smart to buy roasts when they are on special, then keep them in your freezer. Here's a method for foil-roasting frozen roasts that keeps in those luscious beef juices.

Place a large sheet of heavy-duty aluminum foil on a rack in a shallow roasting pan. Place a 4-pound frozen, rolled (not bone-in) roast in the center of the foil. Bring the foil up over the top and seal with a double fold; leave the ends open. Roast at 400° for 1 hour. Open foil; brush meat with salad oil and sprinkle with salt and pepper. Reseal foil over top; cook 1 hour more. Open fold and crumple foil to fit sides of meat loosely, leaving top exposed. Brush again with salad oil. Roast 30 to 60 minutes more or until brown and done to your preference. Allow 40 minutes per pound for medium rare. Makes 6 servings.

❀ Saucy Short Ribs

2½ to 3 pounds lean beef
   short ribs
2 teaspoons salt
⅛ teaspoon pepper
2 medium potatoes, pared
   and quartered
1 medium onion, sliced

½ cup sliced celery
1 tablespoon chopped
   parsley
1 tablespoon prepared
   horseradish
2 (8 oz.) cans tomato sauce
   with mushrooms

Cut beef into serving-size pieces; trim fat. Sprinkle with salt and pepper; place in casserole. Brown meat, uncovered, in 400° oven for 1 hour. Remove fat. Add remaining ingredients. Cover and bake at 375° ½ hour longer, or until tender. Makes 4 servings.

❀ *Savory Chuck Steak*

3 *pounds blade chuck roast,* 1 *medium onion, sliced*
 cut about 2 inches thick 2½ *cups water*
salt   1 *(2⅜ oz.) package beef*
pepper   *with barley and vegetable*
flour   *dry-soup mix*
2 *tablespoons soft*
 shortening

Season meat with salt and pepper and sprinkle with flour to coat
lightly. Heat shortening in large saucepan or Dutch oven over moderate heat. Brown meat thoroughly on both sides; add onion during
the last few minutes and brown lightly. Heat oven to 325°. Stir
water slowly into dry-soup mix and pour over and under meat.
Cover and place in oven; cook about 2 hours, or until fork tender.
If necessary, add a little water during cooking to prevent sticking.
Slice meat and serve with pan gravy. Makes 6 to 8 servings.

❀ *Savory Sweet-Sour Short Ribs*

4 *pounds beef short ribs, cut* 1½ *cups water*
 in serving pieces   1 *onion, sliced*
3 *tablespoons flour*   1 *cup sliced celery*
2 *teaspoons salt*   1 *(8¼ oz.) can sliced*
¼ *teaspoon pepper*   *pineapple, with liquid*
2 *tablespoons salad oil*   1½ *cups ketchup*

Roll short ribs in flour, salt, and pepper; brown in oil in large skillet.
Add water; bring to boil. Cover and simmer 2 hours, or until tender.
Pour off liquid, reserving 1 cup; return to skillet with meat. Add
onion, celery, pineapple, and ketchup. Cook, covered, 30 minutes.
Thicken gravy with cornstarch, if desired. Serve with rice, if de-
sired. Makes 6 to 8 servings.

❀ *Sirloin Tip with Noodles*

2 pounds sirloin tip, or 3
   pounds chuck arm steak
2 tablespoons flour
1 to 2 teaspoons chili
   powder
1 teaspoon salt
⅛ teaspoon pepper

¼ cup salad oil
2 cups water
1 medium onion, chopped
½ cup chopped green
   pepper
1 (8 oz.) package noodles

Trim fat from meat; cut meat in strips about 2 by ½ inch. Toss meat with flour, chili powder, salt, and pepper. In skillet brown meat in salad oil. Stir in tomato paste, water, onion, and green pepper. Simmer, covered, about 1 hour, or until meat is tender. Meanwhile, cook noodles and drain; keep hot. Arrange noodles on serving platter; spoon meat and sauce over. Makes 6 servings.

❀ *Smothered Chuck Steak*

3 pounds chuck steak, 1½
   inches thick
instant meat tenderizer
1 tablespoon salad oil
2 large onions, thinly sliced
1 teaspoon salt

⅛ teaspoon pepper
1 teaspoon dried oregano
1 teaspoon dried parsley
2 tablespoons lemon juice
1 tablespoon chili sauce
¼ cup water

Sprinkle steak with meat tenderizer as directed on jar. Pierce steak at 1-inch intervals with cooking fork. Heat oil in large, heavy skillet over moderate heat. Add steak and brown about 3 minutes on each side. Remove steak; add onions and cook over low heat until golden brown. Add salt, pepper, oregano, parsley, lemon juice, chili sauce, and water. Bring to boil; add browned steak. Simmer gently 10 to 15 minutes for rare, a few minutes longer for medium well. Slice diagonally across the grain and serve with onion mixture. Makes 6 to 8 servings.

❀ Stuffed Round Steak

4 slices bacon, diced
1 onion, chopped
1½ cups toasted bread
　cubes
2 tablespoons minced
　parsley
½ teaspoon celery salt

¼ teaspoon sage
2 to 2½ pounds thin round
　steak
½ teaspoon salt
⅛ teaspoon pepper
1½ cups bouillon or beef
　broth

To make stuffing, cook bacon with onion; mix in bread cubes, parsley, celery salt, and sage. Sprinkle steak with salt and pepper. Fold meat to form a pocket; fill with stuffing and fasten with toothpicks or small skewers. Place in large skillet. Pour bouillon over; cover and simmer 1½ hours. Makes 6 to 8 servings.

❀ Swiss Pepper Steak

1 blade-bone chuck steak, 1
　inch thick (about 3½
　lbs.)
2 tablespoons salad oil
4 green peppers, cut into
　strips
2 large onions, sliced
salt
pepper

1 (1 lb.) can tomatoes, with
　liquid
1 (8 oz.) can tomato sauce
8 sprigs parsley
2 celery leaves
1 beef bouillon cube,
　crumbled
1 bay leaf

Preheat oven to 350°. Wipe steak with damp paper towels. In hot oil in Dutch oven brown steak on each side; remove. Arrange half the green pepper strips and half the onion slices in Dutch oven, sprinkle with ¾ teaspoon salt and ¼ teaspoon pepper. Place steak on top. Cover with remaining green pepper and onion; sprinkle lightly with salt and pepper. Add tomatoes, tomato sauce, parsley, celery leaves, bouillon cube, and bay leaf. Bake, covered, 2 hours, or until steak is tender. Remove steak from Dutch oven and place on heated serving platter. Pour all liquid into a 2-cup measure, skim off fat, and discard. Add enough water to liquid to make 1 cup. Pour over steak. Makes 6 servings.

❀ Swiss Steak Skillet

1½ pounds boneless round   2 tablespoons salad oil
   or chuck steak, 1 inch   1 onion, sliced
   thick   1 clove garlic, minced
2 tablespoons flour   2 cups water
1½ teaspoons salt   1 cup celery, sliced
¼ teaspoon pepper   3 carrots, sliced

Combine flour, salt, and pepper; pound into both sides of steak with mallet or edge of plate. Cut steak into serving-size pieces. Brown in salad oil in large skillet. Pour off excess fat. Add onion, garlic, and water. Cover and simmer 1½ hours. Add celery and carrots; continue simmering 45 minutes. Makes 6 servings.

❀ Tamale Pie

2 tablespoons shortening   ¼ cup coarsely chopped
1 cup coarsely chopped   stuffed green olives
   onion   2 teaspoons sugar
1 cup chopped green   2 teaspoons chili powder
   pepper   1 teaspoon salt
1 (12 oz.) can whole kernel   few grains pepper
   corn, drained   2 cups coarsely chopped
2 (8 oz.) cans tomato sauce   leftover cooked beef
   with cheese   Corn Bread Topping

Melt shortening in skillet; add onion and green pepper and cook over moderate heat until tender. Add corn, tomato sauce, olives, sugar, chili powder, salt, and pepper; mix well. Combine tomato sauce mixture with meat; pour into shallow 2-quart baking dish. Heat oven to 425°. Prepare Corn Bread Topping and pour over meat mixture. Bake 20 minutes, or until topping is lightly browned. Makes 4 servings.

CORN BREAD TOPPING: Stir together ⅔ cup sifted all-purpose flour, ⅔ cup yellow corn meal, 1 tablespoon baking powder, 2 tablespoons sugar, and ½ teaspoon salt. Add 1 egg, slightly beaten, ½ cup milk, and 2 tablespoons salad oil; beat with rotary beater until smooth, about 1 minute.

❀ *Western Round Steak*

2 pounds round steak, cut in   2 teaspoons chili powder
    serving pieces   ¼ cup salad oil
1 teaspoon salt   1 medium onion, sliced
¼ teaspoon pepper   1 green pepper, sliced
1 egg, beaten   2 (8 oz.) cans tomato sauce
1 cup finely crushed corn   with mushrooms
    flakes   1 cup water

Trim fat off steak; pound meat. Sprinkle with salt and pepper. Dip
first in egg, then in corn flakes mixed with chili powder. Brown
meat on both sides in salad oil at medium heat. Add remaining
ingredients. Cover and simmer 45 to 60 minutes. Makes 6 servings.

❀ *Baked Lamb Chops*

4 shoulder lamb chops   1 (16 oz.) can stewed
    (about 2¼ lbs.)   tomatoes
salt   ½ teaspoon dried basil
½ cup coarsely chopped   1 teaspoon salt
    onion   ⅛ teaspoon pepper
½ cup coarsely chopped
    green pepper

Remove as much fat as possible from chops. Heat oven to 350°.
Heat a medium-size skillet over moderately high heat and sprinkle
bottom with salt. Brown chops on both sides. Remove chops from
skillet and arrange in a shallow 2-quart baking dish. Reduce heat
to moderately low. Add onion and green pepper to skillet and cook
until tender, stirring occasionally. Add tomatoes, basil, 1 teaspoon
salt, and pepper; heat until boiling. Remove from heat and pour
over chops. Bake 1 hour or until chops are tender. Makes 4 servings.

❀ Baked Lamb and Rice

1 tablespoon olive oil
1¾ pounds lamb, cut into
    1-inch cubes
1 medium onion, sliced
½ cup chopped green
    pepper
1 cup uncooked rice
½ teaspoon oregano

¼ teaspoon basil
¼ teaspoon paprika
1½ teaspoons salt
⅛ teaspoon pepper
2 beef bouillon cubes
2½ cups boiling water
1 (8 oz.) can tomato sauce

Heat oil in skillet; add meat cubes and cook over moderate heat until lightly browned on all sides. Remove meat from skillet. Add onion and green pepper and cook until just tender. Add rice, oregano, basil, paprika, salt, and pepper; cook over low heat until lightly browned. Heat oven to 350°. Mix meat and rice together and spoon into a 1½-quart buttered casserole. Dissolve bouillon cubes in boiling water; stir in tomato sauce. Pour enough of the liquid into casserole to barely cover rice. Cover and bake 1¼ to 1½ hours, stirring every 15 minutes; add remaining bouillon mixture as liquid is absorbed. When all the bouillon mixture has been used, add boiling water if necessary. Makes 4 to 6 servings.

❀ Currant-Glazed Lamb Leg Chops

2 tablespoons butter or
    margarine
4 lamb leg chops, cut ½
    inch thick (about 1½
    lbs.)
salt
pepper

½ cup water
¼ cup currant jelly
1 tablespoon lemon juice
2 tablespoons dark brown
    sugar
¼ teaspoon ground ginger
¼ teaspoon ground cloves

Heat butter in skillet; add chops and brown well on both sides over moderate heat. Sprinkle with salt and pepper. Remove chops from skillet. Add water, jelly, lemon juice, brown sugar, ginger, and cloves; mix until blended. Return chops; cover and cook 30 to 35 minutes, until fork tender. Add a little more water to prevent sticking if necessary. Makes 4 servings.

❀ Curried Lamb and Beans

2 cups dried pea beans
water
3 tablespoons salad oil
2 pounds shoulder of lamb,
    cut into 1½-inch cubes

½ cup sliced onion
2 teaspoons salt
1 to 1½ tablespoons curry
    powder
⅓ cup chopped chutney

Wash beans, turn into medium bowl, and cover with cold water. Refrigerate, covered, overnight. Next day, drain beans. In large saucepan, cover beans with 6 cups of water; bring to boil. Reduce heat; simmer, covered, 45 to 55 minutes, or until beans are tender. Drain beans, reserving 2¼ cups cooking liquid. Meanwhile, in hot oil in Dutch oven or heavy skillet with tight-fitting lid, brown meat well. Remove meat. In same skillet, sauté onion until tender (about 5 minutes). Return meat to skillet. Stir in the reserved cooking liquid, salt, and curry powder; simmer, covered, 45 minutes, stirring occasionally. Add beans; simmer, covered, 30 minutes longer. Stir in chutney. Makes 4 to 6 servings.

❀ Lamb Breast with Orange Curry Sauce

3 pounds breast of lamb,
    cut into 3-inch squares
salt
pepper
1 tablespoon cornstarch
1 teaspoon curry powder

2 tablespoons sugar
1 cup orange juice
¼ cup lemon juice
4 cups hot cooked rice
2 oranges, peeled and sliced
    ½ inch thick

Heat oven to 350°. Arrange lamb pieces on rack in shallow baking pan; sprinkle with salt and pepper. Bake about 1 hour, or until meat is fork tender. Combine cornstarch, curry powder, and sugar in small saucepan. Gradually stir in orange juice and lemon juice. Cook over low heat, stirring constantly, until clear and slightly thickened. Put hot rice on serving platter; arrange lamb pieces on rice; garnish with orange slices. Pour hot sauce over all. Makes 6 servings.

❧ Lamb Hot Pot

2 pounds small white
   potatoes, pared and sliced
   ¼ inch thick
2 pounds lamb shoulder,
   cut into 1½-inch cubes
1 large onion, sliced
2 cups sliced carrots

2 teaspoons salt
½ teaspoon pepper
1 cup canned chicken broth
2 tablespoons butter or
   margarine, melted
1 (10½ oz.) can chicken
   gravy

Preheat oven to 350°. Grease well a 3-quart Dutch oven and layer half the potatoes in it. Cover with lamb, then sliced onion and carrots. Sprinkle with salt and pepper. Place remaining potatoes, overlapping the slices, on top of carrot layer. Pour broth over all. Brush tops of potato slices with butter and bake, covered, 2 hours. Bake, uncovered, about 50 minutes, or until potatoes are crisp and browned. Meanwhile, heat gravy over low heat. Pour gravy around edge of Dutch oven. Makes 4 to 6 servings.

❧ Lamb Riblets with Orange Sauce

3 pounds lamb riblets, cut
   into 2-rib portions
salt
pepper
2 oranges, sliced and halved
2 medium onions, sliced

1 tablespoon cornstarch
2 tablespoons sugar
dash ground allspice
1 cup orange juice
2 tablespoons lemon juice

Heat oven to 400°. Arrange lamb riblets on rack in shallow baking pan; sprinkle with salt and pepper. Bake about 45 minutes, until lightly browned. Pour off fat and remove rack. Reduce oven temperature to 350°. Arrange lamb riblets in bottom of pan and place orange and onion slices between and on top of lamb pieces, reserving a few pieces of orange for garnish. Bake about 1½ hours, or until lamb is fork tender. Combine cornstarch, sugar, and allspice in saucepan. Gradually stir in orange and lemon juices. Cook over low heat until thickened and clear, stirring constantly. At serving time, arrange lamb riblets on platter. Discard cooked onion and orange slices. Pour orange sauce over lamb. Garnish with reserved orange slices. Makes 4 to 6 servings.

❀ Lemony Lamb Shanks

3 *lamb shanks*
5 *tablespoons flour*
1 *teaspoon salt*
½ *teaspoon pepper*
½ *teaspoon paprika*
2 *tablespoons shortening or
  salad oil*

1¾ *cups water*
2 *tablespoons grated lemon
  rind*
½ *cup lemon juice*
2 *bay leaves*
4 *whole black peppers*
1 *clove garlic*

For quicker cooking and easier serving, have butcher crack bones in lamb shanks. Combine 4 tablespoons flour, salt, pepper, and paprika; coat lamb with this mixture. In Dutch oven or heavy skillet, heat salad oil. Add lamb shanks; brown thoroughly, turning often. Add 1½ cups water and remaining ingredients, except flour. Bring to boil then reduce heat; cover and simmer slowly for 1½ to 2 hours, or until lamb is tender. Transfer to serving platter and keep warm. Meanwhile, skim fat from liquid in pan. Make a smooth paste of remaining 1 tablespoon flour and ¼ cup water. Blend into pan liquid; cook, stirring, until gravy boils and is thick and smooth. Pour over lamb shanks. Makes 4 to 6 servings.

❀ Pineapple Shish Kebab

2 *pounds boneless lamb
  shoulder*
6 *tablespoons lemon juice*
4 *tablespoons salad oil*
1 *tablespoon grated onion*
1 *teaspoon chili powder*
1 *teaspoon ground ginger*
1 *clove garlic, crushed*

2 *teaspoons curry powder*
3 *teaspoons salt*
1 *green pepper, cut into
  2-inch squares*
2 *onions, cut into eighths*
1 (8 oz.) *can pineapple
  chunks, drained*

Cut lamb into 1½-inch cubes. Combine lemon juice, salad oil, onion, chili powder, ginger, garlic, curry powder, and salt. Pour mixture over lamb cubes. Cover and refrigerate at least 2 hours. Preheat broiler. Drain meat and reserve marinade. Arrange meat on metal skewers alternately with green pepper squares, onion, and pineapple chunks. Place on broiler rack 3 inches from heat. Broil about 15 minutes, turning frequently to brown evenly on all sides. Baste

several times with the marinade during broiling. Serve with rice.
Makes 4 to 6 servings.

❀ *Mock Chicken Legs*

1 pound ground veal shoulder	*¼ teaspoon ground rosemary*
1 teaspoon salt	*1 egg, slightly beaten*
dash pepper	*⅓ cup fine dry bread crumbs*
2 tablespoons chopped parsley	*3 tablespoons butter or margarine*
2 tablespoons melted butter or margarine	*1 cup commercial sour cream*

Combine veal, salt, pepper, parsley, melted butter, rosemary, and
egg. Mix lightly. Divide mixture into 4 equal portions. Shape each
portion around a metal or wooden skewer to look like a chicken leg.
Roll each in bread crumbs, being careful to coat well on all sides.
Heat 3 tablespoons butter in a skillet over moderate heat. When
butter bubbles, put in meat. Cook, turning frequently to prevent
meat from sticking, until meat is well browned, about 15 minutes.
Use tongs or 2 tablespoons to turn meat easily. Cover tightly and
cook over low heat 10 minutes. Remove meat to a heated platter
and keep warm. Add sour cream to drippings in skillet. Stir to
loosen brown particles from bottom of skillet. Heat until cream is
very hot but not boiling. Pour over meat. Makes 3 servings.

❀ *Osso Buco*

3 veal shanks, each quartered	*1 cup chopped celery*
3 tablespoons flour	*1 cup thinly sliced carrot*
1 teaspoon salt	*¼ cup tomato paste*
¼ teaspoon pepper	*2 cups white wine*
¼ cup salad oil	*2 bay leaves*
1 clove garlic, crushed	*¼ cup finely chopped parsley*
1 cup sliced onion	

Wipe veal with damp paper towels. Combine flour with salt and
pepper; use to coat veal well. Gently heat oil in large heavy skillet
or Dutch oven. Over medium heat brown veal well, turning on all

sides; this takes 20 minutes in all. Remove veal as it browns. Add garlic, onion, celery, and carrot to skillet, sauté until onion is golden brown, about 5 minutes. Combine tomato paste with wine; stir into sautéed vegetables along with bay leaves and chopped parsley. Return veal to skillet; simmer over low heat, covered, 1¾ to 2 hours, or until veal is tender. When serving, spoon pan liquid over veal, garnish with lemon slices if desired, and accompany with a mixture of peas and rice. Makes 4 to 6 servings.

❀ Rolled Breast of Veal

1 breast of veal, boned (5 to 6 lbs.)	1½ cups fine dry bread crumbs
3 tablespoons butter or margarine	1 teaspoon dried thyme
1 large onion, finely chopped	½ teaspoon salt
1 clove garlic, finely minced	2 eggs, slightly beaten
1 cup bulk sausage	¼ cup fresh chopped parsley
3 tablespoons milk	3 strips bacon

Spread meat out as flat as possible. Heat butter in heavy saucepan over low heat. Add onion and garlic; cook until onion is soft. Break up sausage with a fork; add to onion and cook 5 minutes. Add milk, bread crumbs, thyme, salt, eggs, and parsley. Blend thoroughly. Spread stuffing mixture over surface of veal; starting with the wide side, roll up carefully and tie securely with string. Place roll on rack in shallow baking pan. Lay bacon strips over top. Heat oven to 325°. Roast veal 25 minutes per pound, or until a meat thermometer inserted in the center registers 165°. Makes 6 to 8 servings.

❀ Veal and Peppers

4 medium green peppers	2 cups canned tomatoes
2 tablespoons salad oil	1 teaspoon salt
1 medium onion, sliced	pepper
1 pound veal, cut into 1-inch cubes	6 tablespoons dry white wine

Wash, stem, and seed green peppers; cut each into six sections. Heat 1 tablespoon oil in skillet over low heat; add onion and green peppers and cook until tender, stirring frequently. Remove onion and peppers. Add and heat the remaining tablespoon of oil over moderately high heat; add veal and cook until lightly browned, stirring occasionally. Add tomatoes, salt, and pepper; cover and cook over low heat 30 minutes. Add green peppers, onion, and wine; cover and cook 30 minutes. Makes 4 servings.

❀ Veal en Brochette

1 *pound boneless veal*	*melted butter or margarine*
shoulder	*salt*
1 *(4 oz.) can mushroom*	1 *(17 oz.) can fruits for*
buttons	*salad, drained*

Cut veal into 1½-inch squares. On long metal skewers alternate meat squares and mushrooms. Brush with butter. Sprinkle meat lightly with salt. Arrange on rack in broiler pan. Place in preheated broiler about 4 inches from heat. Broil 10 minutes; turn and brush with butter. Thread fruit pieces on metal skewers; brush with butter and place on broiler rack with meat. Continue to broil 5 minutes. Makes 4 servings.

❀ Veal Patties with Pineapple

1 *tablespoon instant minced*	½ *teaspoon seasoned salt*
onion	1 *(8½ oz.) can sliced*
1 *tablespoon water*	*pineapple*
2 *cups ground leftover*	3 *tablespoons dark brown*
cooked veal	*sugar*
¾ *cup commercial sour*	3 *tablespoons butter or*
cream	*margarine*
1 *egg, slightly beaten*	*pinch ground cloves*
1 *cup fine dry bread crumbs*	
2 *tablespoons dried parsley*	
flakes	

Heat oven to 425°. Mix onion and water together and let stand 1 minute. Mix this with ground veal, sour cream, egg, bread crumbs, parsley, and seasoned salt; shape into 4 patties about 1½ inches thick. Drain pineapple, reserving juice. Mix pineapple juice, brown sugar, butter, and cloves in small saucepan; heat until butter and sugar are blended. Place pineapple rings in shallow 1½-quart baking dish; top each with a pattie. Pour sauce over patties. Bake 25 minutes; baste occasionally. Makes 2 to 3 servings.

❊ Veal Pot Roast with Mushroom Sauce

4 pounds rolled, boned
  shoulder of veal
1 tablespoon paprika
2 teaspoons salt
4 tablespoons salad oil
½ cup chopped onion

1 (10½ oz.) can condensed
  golden mushroom soup,
  undiluted
3 tablespoons flour
2 tablespoons water
½ cup commercial sour
  cream

Wipe veal with damp paper towels. Rub with paprika and salt. Preheat oven to 350°. In hot oil in Dutch oven brown veal well, then remove. Add onion to pan drippings; sauté until golden, about 5 minutes. Stir in soup. Return veal to pan. Bake, covered, 2½ hours, or until veal is tender. Remove veal to serving platter; keep warm. Skim fat from liquid in Dutch oven. Mix flour with water. Gradually stir into liquid in Dutch oven; bring to boil, stirring. Reduce heat; simmer 3 minutes. In small bowl, gradually stir a little hot gravy into sour cream, then stir this into rest of gravy. Pour into gravy boat and serve with veal. Makes 8 servings.

❊ Veal Riblets and Noodles

⅓ cup flour
1¼ teaspoons paprika
1½ teaspoons salt
⅛ teaspoon pepper
2 to 2½ pounds veal riblets
3 tablespoons vegetable oil
1 can condensed cream of
  mushroom soup

¾ cup milk
1 clove garlic, finely
  chopped
1 cup thinly sliced onion
½ teaspoon salt
2 tablespoons chili sauce
8 ounces noodles, cooked

Place flour, paprika, 1½ teaspoons salt, and pepper in plastic or paper bag. Shake riblets, a few pieces at a time, in bag until coated with flour mixture. Heat oil in Dutch oven or heavy saucepan; add riblets and cook over moderate heat until browned. Combine soup, milk, garlic, onion, and ½ teaspoon salt; pour over riblets. Cover and cook over low heat 2 hours, or until fork tender, stirring constantly. Skim off fat and stir in chili sauce. Serve over hot cooked noodles. Makes 4 servings.

HAM AND PORK

It is entirely possible that hieroglyphics would be easier to understand than the nomenclature of ham. Ham is never just ham—it is whole ham, shank half, butt half, country or aged ham, uncooked, precooked, tenderized, or canned ham. And as if that were not confusion enough, there are picnic and cottage hams, which to the eye at least don't resemble their names.

Let's sort them out and see which might be the wise choice for the shopper who is trying to manage her household accounts so skillfully that her husband will treat her to an expensive dinner out.

By definition, a ham comes from the rear leg of a hog; it is cut from the hipbone through the meaty part of the shank. A whole ham can weigh from 14 to 18 pounds and wears a premium price tag. Cut in half as they most often are, a whole ham produces a shank (or lower) half and a butt (or upper) half. Both halves are fine, but the shank half is more economical. With the shank half you can get a piece for boiling, a piece for baking, and slices for frying. You can even put the bone to good use by making pea soup with it. The butt half can be used for frying and boiling, but baking is its primary use. Because it has less waste, less fat, less bone, and more meat, it will cost more. So, for real economy buy a half ham (usually 5 to 8 pounds) and have one or two ham slices cut off. Ham slices bought separately are always more expensive per pound.

Country or aged ham is ham cured and smoked by a long, slow process—the hams are hung at least a year—and accordingly the price can hang high, too. Virginia, Smithfield, and Kentucky hams are traditional examples of these specially cured hams.

Most hams produced by national packing houses have been mildly cured or smoked. Buy them either uncooked (actually they are partially tenderized) or fully cooked (precooked). Such hams are supposed to be ready for eating, but you will find their flavor and texture improved by heating them through.

Canned hams are thoroughly cooked and need only to be heated. Since they are perishable, they should be stored in the refrigerator even while they are in the can. In addition to United States varieties, there are many canned hams from Poland, Denmark, Germany, the Netherlands, and other countries. Naturally, imported brands can be more expensive than home-grown ones.

For the ham lover, there are also ham hocks, which offer a real ham flavor and are perfect in soups, stews, and combination dishes. And they are delightfully inexpensive.

Other cuts of cured, smoked pork often called "ham" actually come from the shoulder. Categorized as picnic hams, they are most frequently labeled smoked pork shoulder or pork shoulder roll or butt. These shoulder cuts have slightly more fat than ham cut from the leg bone, so you must plan servings accordingly. The cut known as smoked Boston shoulder roll or boneless pork cottage roll tastes very much like ham but has virtually no waste. You can roast, braise, broil, pan broil, or pan fry a cottage roll. Slices of a cottage roll will be close in flavor to Canadian bacon but are far more economical.

An admirable quality of ham is its total usefulness—you do not have to throw away any part of it. Leftover ham can be ground for ham loaf and ham patties, used for Eggs Benedict or casseroles, or added to cream sauces. And as we mentioned previously, even the bone can have its moment of glory as a flavorsome part of pea soup.

Few meats offer the versatility and flavor variety of pork. Thanks to present-day standards set by meat producers, packers, and retailers, pork cuts contain more edible meat per pound than ever before, more body-building proteins, and less fat. Pork actually is a nutritional powerhouse; in addition to its protein content, it is a major source of iron and B vitamins.

Like beef, pork boasts a broad spectrum of cuts at varying price levels. A pork tenderloin is an expensive cut, but there is no waste and it can be roasted whole, stuffed, or sliced. A pork loin roast is also a choice selection, as are loin and rib chops. Look for cuts from the shoulder area for the real bargains. Shoulder blade steaks can be prepared just like the more expensive pork chops. The blade loin roast—from the end of the loin nearest the shoulder—has more bone in it and may be somewhat difficult to carve, but it, too, is far less costly.

There is no need to recommend spareribs, which have long been a mainstay of the provident cook. Spareribs are always a welcome meal, flavorful, appetizing, and fun to eat. Don't overlook country- or farm-style spareribs. These offer more servings per pound than regular spareribs because they have more meat on them. They are prepared the same way as any spareribs.

In choosing any pork, look for fine-grained flesh, firm white fat, and bones of a pinkish color. And cook until well done.

A final word about pork: you can eat it even when you're count- ing calories. A three-ounce serving of roast pork butt with the fat trimmed off, for example, contains approximately 205 calories. That should be good news for the bored-with-burgers dieter.

❀ *Baked Ham Tetrazzini*

1 pound spaghetti, broken into 2-inch pieces

2 cans condensed cream of mushroom soup

2 cups milk

1 tablespoon finely chopped onion

2 cups shredded sharp Cheddar cheese

½ teaspoon salt

¼ teaspoon pepper

2 teaspoons Worcestershire sauce

¼ cup fresh chopped parsley

¼ cup chopped pimiento

3 cups cubed baked ham

Cook spaghetti in boiling salted water as directed on package; drain. Heat oven to 375°. Combine soup and milk; stir until smooth. Add remaining ingredients except ham. Pour soup mixture over cooked spaghetti and toss to coat evenly. Arrange layers of spaghetti mix- ture and cubed ham in a greased 2½-quart casserole. Bake 30 min- utes until thoroughly heated and bubbly around the edge. Makes 4 to 6 servings.

❀ Country Boiled Dinner

1 fully cooked ham shank
  (6 lbs.)
½ pound small white
  onions, peeled
whole cloves
1 pound carrots, pared and
  cut in 2-inch lengths
2 pounds small potatoes,
  pared
4 sprigs parsley

1 teaspoon salt
¼ teaspoon pepper
¼ teaspoon dried thyme
  leaves
1 bay leaf
1 (13¾ oz.) can chicken
  broth
1 (2 lb.) head cabbage, cut
  in 6 wedges

Preheat oven to 350°. Trim fat and rind from ham. Coarsely chop
2 onions; place in deep roasting pan. Stick cloves in remaining
onions and place in pan along with carrots, potatoes, and ham. Add
parsley, salt, pepper, thyme, and bay leaf. Pour chicken broth over
all. Bake, covered, 1 hour. Arrange cabbage wedges in pan; bake,
covered, 30 minutes longer. To serve, arrange ham on large heated
platter, surround with onions, carrots, potatoes, and cabbage wedges.
Spoon pan juices over all. Makes 6 servings.

❀ Ham à la King

1 (1 lb.) can fully cooked
  ham
3 tablespoons butter or
  margarine
3 tablespoons flour
dash salt
2½ cups milk
few drops liquid hot-pepper
  seasoning

½ teaspoon Worcestershire
  sauce
1 cup grated Swiss cheese
  (¼ lb.)
3 tablespoons drained
  sweet pickle relish
3 tablespoons drained
  chopped pimiento

Remove and discard gelatine and excess fat from ham. Cut ham into
½-inch cubes. Set aside. Melt butter in medium saucepan; remove
from heat. Stir in flour and salt. Gradually stir in milk. Add hot-
pepper seasoning and Worcestershire. Bring to boil, stirring occasionally. Remove from heat. Add cheese, stirring until melted. Add
ham, pickle relish, and pimiento. Cook over very low heat, stirring,
until heated through. Serve over toast, waffles, or toasted English
muffins. Makes 4 1-cup servings.

❃ Ham and Sweet Potatoes

3 fully cooked, boneless
    ham slices, ½ inch thick
    (about 2 lbs.)
2 tablespoons prepared
    mustard
¾ cup light brown sugar,
    firmly packed

1 (1 lb. 1 oz.) can pear
    halves, drained
1 (1 lb. 1 oz.) can sweet
    potatoes, drained and
    halved
2 tablespoons butter or
    margarine

Preheat oven to 400°. Cut each ham slice in half; place each half
in center of large piece of heavy-duty foil. Combine mustard and ½
cup brown sugar. Spread on ham slices. Arrange pears and sweet
potatoes on top of ham and sprinkle with rest of brown sugar; dot
with butter. Fold ends of foil over each to make a packet. Place on
cookie sheet and bake 30 minutes, or until heated through. Makes
6 servings.

❃ Ham Hash in Zucchini Shells

2 medium zucchini
½ teaspoon salt
1 cup finely chopped
    cooked ham (4 oz.)
1 cup finely chopped
    cooked potato
3 tablespoons mayonnaise

3 tablespoons finely
    chopped green pepper
2 tablespoons finely
    chopped onion
dash pepper
2 slices process American
    cheese, cut in strips

Wash zucchini well, scrubbing with vegetable brush, and halve
lengthwise. In skillet bring 1 inch of water to boil. Add salt. Place
zucchini, cut side down, in water. Simmer uncovered 10 to 15 minutes, or until tender but not mushy. Drain. Preheat oven to 350°.
Meanwhile, make Ham Hash: in medium bowl combine remaining
ingredients (except cheese) and mix until well blended. Carefully
scoop pulp from zucchini, leaving shells ¼ inch thick. Add pulp to
hash. Fill zucchini shells with hash, mounding high. Cover with
cheese strips. Place shells on cookie sheet. Bake, uncovered, 15 minutes, or until cheese is melted and hash is hot. Makes 2 servings.

❀ Ham Hocks and Cabbage

2 to 2½ pounds smoked
   ham hocks
1½ quarts water
1 teaspoon salt
1 bay leaf
1 (6 oz.) can tomato paste

2 potatoes, pared and
   quartered
1 small head cabbage,
   quartered
1 small onion, quartered

In kettle or Dutch oven combine ham hocks, water, salt, and bay leaf. Simmer, covered, about 1½ hours, or until tender. Remove skin and bones from meat; skim fat from broth. Return meat to broth along with remaining ingredients. Simmer 20 to 25 minutes more, or until vegetables are tender. Makes 4 servings.

❀ Ham-Rice Toss

1 cup chopped ham
½ cup chopped onion
½ cup chopped green
   pepper
½ cup sliced celery

1 cup raw regular rice
2 tablespoons salad oil
2 (8 oz.) cans tomato sauce
1 cup water
½ teaspoon salt

Cook ham, onion, green pepper, celery, and rice in salad oil until vegetables soften; stir constantly. Add tomato sauce, water, and salt. Cover and simmer 25 to 30 minutes, until liquid is absorbed and rice is done. Makes 4 servings.

❀ Ham Steak Boulangère

3 fully cooked ham slices,
   about ½ inch thick
8 small potatoes, pared
8 small onions, peeled
2 cloves garlic, halved
¾ cup apple juice

1½ teaspoons seasoned salt
4 whole allspice
2 whole cloves
1 (10 oz.) package frozen
   Brussels sprouts, thawed

Preheat oven to 350°. Wipe ham with damp paper towels. Trim a little fat from ham and place in 3-quart casserole. Cut each ham slice in half. Layer ham slices, potatoes, onions, and garlic in casserole. Combine apple juice, seasoned salt, allspice, and cloves; pour into casserole. Bake, covered, 1¼ to 1½ hours, or until potatoes are just tender. Add Brussels sprouts; bake, covered, 20 minutes or until sprouts are tender. Makes 6 servings.

🏵 *Apricot Smoked-Pork Shoulder*

1 boneless smoked pork shoulder (3 lbs.)	⅛ teaspoon ground thyme
2 tablespoons apricot jam, mixed with 2 tablespoons water	1 tablespoon chopped parsley
	2 tablespoons melted butter or margarine
1½ cups soft bread crumbs	2 tablespoons apricot jam
¼ teaspoon ground sage	1 teaspoon light corn syrup

Remove wrappings from meat. Place in a large saucepan; cover with water. Cover and simmer 1½ hours. Drain and cool slightly. Preheat oven to 400°. Make a deep lengthwise cut in meat. Combine apricot jam and water mixture with bread crumbs, sage, thyme, parsley, and butter. Toss lightly. Spoon stuffing into cut in meat. Blend apricot jam with corn syrup. Brush this mixture over meat. Bake about 30 minutes, or until stuffing is brown and meat is glazed. Makes 8 to 10 servings.

🏵 *Braised Pork Steaks*

2 tablespoons shortening	⅛ teaspoon ground ginger
2 1-inch-thick pork steaks (about 2 lbs.)	½ teaspoon salt
	1 small green pepper, thinly sliced
1 (13½ oz.) can pineapple chunks	1 tablespoon cornstarch
2 tablespoons vinegar	2 tablespoons water
1 tablespoon soy sauce	hot cooked rice
2 teaspoons sugar	

Melt shortening in skillet; brown steaks on both sides over moderate heat. Remove steaks; drain fat from skillet. Drain pineapple, reserving juice. Mix pineapple juice, vinegar, soy sauce, sugar, ginger, and salt in skillet, add steaks. Cover and cook over very low heat. Add pineapple chunks and green pepper; cover and cook 15 to 20 minutes, or until steaks are fork tender. Blend cornstarch and water together; gradually stir into juices in skillet. Cook over moderate heat until thickened, stirring constantly. Serve with hot cooked rice. Makes 4 servings.

❀ *Chops and Beans*

6 *loin pork chops (about ½*   2 *tablespoons brown sugar*
  inch thick), trimmed   1 *tablespoon vinegar*
2 *tablespoons salad oil*   ½ *teaspoon sage*
1 *small onion, chopped*   ¼ *teaspoon salt*
½ *cup chopped green*   1 *(15½ oz.) can red kidney*
  pepper   *beans, drained*
1 *clove garlic, minced*   1 *(10 oz.) package frozen*
2 *(8 oz.) cans tomato sauce*   *baby lima beans, thawed*
  with cheese

In large skillet brown chops in salad oil; remove from skillet. Add onion, green pepper, and garlic; cook until tender. Pour off fat. Stir in tomato sauce, brown sugar, vinegar, sage, and salt. Add pork chops; simmer, covered, 30 minutes. Stir in beans; simmer, covered, 20 minutes more. Makes 3 to 4 servings.

❀ *Dinner Chops and Rice*

6 *pork chops (½ inch*   2 *cups water*
  thick)   1 *tablespoon sugar*
salt   1½ *teaspoons salt*
pepper   1 *(6 oz.) can tomato paste*
2 *tablespoons salad oil*   1 *cup uncooked rice*
1 *onion, chopped*   1 *(10 oz.) package frozen*
½ *cup sliced celery*   *peas, thawed*

Sprinkle pork chops with salt and pepper. Brown in salad oil in skillet. Remove chops. Brown onion and celery in same skillet. Add water, sugar, salt, and tomato paste. Bring to boil. Stir in rice. Place chops on top. Cover tightly; simmer 30 minutes. Add the thawed peas. Cover and simmer 15 minutes more. Makes 3 to 4 servings.

❀ Glazed Shoulder Roast

1 pork shoulder roast (4 to 4½ lbs.)	1 tablespoon brown sugar
salt	1 teaspoon dry mustard
pepper	1 (15 oz.) can pear halves, drained (optional)
½ cup ketchup	

Wipe roast with damp cloth. Place on rack in shallow roasting pan. Sprinkle with salt and pepper. Roast at 350° for about 2½ hours (35 minutes per pound, if roast is at room temperature). One-half hour before roast is done, score top of roast and spoon on glaze of ketchup mixed with brown sugar and mustard. Put pear halves around roast for last 15 minutes, if desired. Makes 6 to 8 servings.

❀ Glazed Smoked Pork

3 pounds boneless smoked pork shoulder butt	2 whole cloves
4 whole black peppers	1 bay leaf
	½ cup apricot preserves

Remove wrapping from pork butt. Place butt in 6-quart kettle or Dutch oven; cover with water. Add peppers, cloves, and bay leaf; bring to boil. Reduce heat and simmer 2¼ hours (45 minutes per pound), or until pork is fork tender. Remove from heat; let meat cool in water about 2 hours. Then preheat oven to 375°. Remove meat from cooking liquid and place in shallow roasting pan. Spread apricot preserves over top. Bake, uncovered, 40 minutes. Serve with buttered carrots and cabbage. Makes 8 to 10 servings.

❀ Hearty Country Ribs

2 to 3 pounds country-style ribs	2 tablespoons brown sugar
salad oil	1 teaspoon prepared mustard
salt	2 (8 oz.) cans tomato sauce
pepper	1 medium onion, thinly sliced
2 tablespoons vinegar	

Brush meat with salad oil. Place in 2-quart baking dish. Sprinkle with salt and pepper. Bake 45 minutes at 400°, turning once. Drain fat.

Combine vinegar, sugar, and mustard; spread on meat. Pour on
tomato sauce, add onions. Cover; bake at 350° for 45 minutes to 1
hour, or until done. Baste occasionally with sauce. Makes 5 to 6
servings.

❀ *Herbed Roast Pork*

1 tablespoon salad oil
1 fresh pork roast, unboned
   (4 to 5 lbs.)
1 cup hot water
1 cup dry sherry
1 clove garlic, finely
   chopped

1 tablespoon dried
   rosemary leaves
1 teaspoon salt
⅛ teaspoon pepper
2 tablespoons flour

Heat oil in ovenproof Dutch oven; add meat and brown on all sides
over moderate heat. Remove from heat. Add water, sherry, garlic,
rosemary, salt, and pepper. Heat oven to 325°. Cover and bake, al-
lowing 45 to 50 minutes per pound. Remove meat to warm platter.
Strain meat juices from Dutch oven into 2-cup measure; skim off all
fat and reserve 2 tablespoons. Spoon the 2 tablespoons fat back
into pot; blend in flour. If necessary, add water to meat juices to
make 1½ cups. Gradually add meat juices to flour mixture and cook
over moderate heat until smooth and thickened, stirring constantly.
Serve gravy with pork. Makes 6 to 8 servings.

❀ *Iowa Skillet Chops*

8 thin pork chops
1 (8 oz.) can tomato sauce
1 tablespoon
   Worcestershire sauce
2 teaspoons instant minced
   onion

1 teaspoon prepared
   mustard
1 (12 oz.) can whole kernel
   corn with sweet peppers,
   drained

In large skillet brown chops; pour off fat. Combine tomato sauce,
Worcestershire, onion, and mustard; stir into corn. Spoon half of
corn mixture over half of chops; top with remaining chops. Spoon
on remaining corn mixture. Simmer, covered, 1 hour, or until chops
are done. Makes 4 servings.

❀ *Oriental Pork and Vegetables*

*1½ to 2 cups julienne strips
   cooked pork roast*
1 cup sliced celery
1 medium onion, sliced
*1 medium green pepper,
   cut in ½-inch pieces*
3 tablespoons salad oil

¾ cup water
⅓ cup soy sauce
1 tablespoon brown sugar
*¼ teaspoon powdered
   ginger*
2 to 3 teaspoons cornstarch

Brown pork and vegetables lightly in salad oil in 12-inch skillet. Stir in ¼ cup water. Cover, cook 10 minutes until vegetables are just crisp-tender. Add soy sauce, sugar, ginger. Blend cornstarch with remaining ½ cup water. Add and cook, stirring until sauce is transparent. Serve over rice. Makes 4 to 5 servings.

❀ *Piggy-Bank Pork Dinner*

*1 boneless pork cottage roll
   (about 2 lbs.)*
1 quart water
12 small boiling onions

6 whole cloves
1 bay leaf
6 yams, pared and halved
Tomato Raisin Sauce

In kettle or Dutch oven place meat, water, onions, cloves, and bay leaf. Simmer, covered, 1 hour; remove bay leaf. Add yams and simmer, covered, 25 minutes more, until meat and vegetables are tender. Arrange on platter. Spoon Tomato Rasin Sauce over. Makes 6 servings.

TOMATO RAISIN SAUCE: In saucepan combine 3 tablespoons brown sugar, 2 teaspoons cornstarch, ⅛ teaspoon cinnamon, and ⅛ teaspoon allspice. Stir in 1 (8 oz.) can tomato sauce, ⅓ cup seedless raisins, and ¼ cup water. Cook, stirring constantly, until thickened and clear, about 3 minutes. Makes about 1½ cups sauce.

❀ *Polish Meatball Casserole*

POTATO BORDER:

    1 (7 oz.) package instant   *2 teaspoons salt*
       mashed potatoes   *1 cup milk*
    ¼ cup margarine

MEATBALLS:

    1½ pounds lean ground   *½ cup finely chopped onion*
       pork   *1½ teaspoons salt*
    1 egg   *½ teaspoon dried marjoram*
    ½ cup packaged   *leaves*
       seasoned dry bread   *¼ teaspoon pepper*
       crumbs   *2 tablespoons flour*
    ½ cup milk   *2 tablespoons salad oil*

SOUR CREAM SAUCE:

    2 tablespoons flour   *parsley*
    1 cup water   *½ cup commercial sour*
    1 beef bouillon cube   *cream*
    ¼ cup grated Parmesan   *2 teaspoons lemon juice*
       cheese

POTATO BORDER: Prepare mashed potatoes as label directs, using amount of water specified on package and the amounts of margarine, salt, and milk listed above. Set aside.

MEATBALLS: In a large bowl combine pork, egg, bread crumbs, milk, onion, salt, marjoram, and pepper; mix lightly until well blended. Shape into balls about 1½ inches in diameter. Preheat oven to 350°. Roll meatballs in flour, coating completely. In hot oil in skillet, sauté meatballs until browned on all sides. Remove, as they brown, to a 2-quart casserole or shallow baking dish; mound in center.

SOUR CREAM SAUCE: Measure drippings in skillet; add more oil, if necessary, to make 2 tablespoons. Return to skillet; stir in flour until smooth. Gradually stir in 1 cup water and the bouillon cube. Bring to boil; remove from heat. Add sour cream and lemon juice, stirring to combine; simmer 2 minutes. Remove from heat.

    Spoon mashed potato around meatballs in casserole; sprinkle potato with cheese. Pour sauce over meatballs. Bake, uncovered, 1

hour, or until potato is golden brown. Garnish with parsley. Makes
8 servings.

❀ *Pork and Macaroni Bake*

1 (8 oz.) package macaroni
1 pound lean ground pork
½ cup chopped onion
½ cup chopped green
  pepper

2 (8 oz.) cans tomato sauce
3 eggs, beaten
½ cup grated carrot
2 tablespoons flour
½ teaspoon salt

Cook macaroni according to package directions; drain well. Sauté
pork, onion, and green pepper until browned. Combine macaroni,
meat mixture, and remaining ingredients. Turn into greased 2-quart
casserole. Bake at 350° for 30 minutes, until bubbly and browned.
Makes 4 servings.

❀ *Pork Chop-Potato Scallop*

6 shoulder pork chops, ½
  inch thick
5 tablespoons flour
1½ teaspoons seasoned salt
½ teaspoon pepper
1½ teaspoons salt
6 medium potatoes, pared
  and thinly sliced

4 medium onions, thinly
  sliced
1 (10¾ oz.) can Cheddar
  cheese soup, undiluted
1½ cups milk

Wipe pork chops with damp paper towels. Trim excess fat and reserve. Combine 3 tablespoons flour, seasoned salt, and ¼ teaspoon
pepper; use to coat chops. Heat fat trimmed from chops in skillet.
Add chops and brown well on both sides, about 20 minutes in all.
Preheat oven to 350°. Meanwhile, combine 2 tablespoons flour,
salt, and ¼ teaspoon pepper. Arrange half of potato slices and half
of onion slices in shallow 3-quart baking dish; sprinkle with half of
flour mixture. Add remaining potato, onion, and flour mixture. In
small saucepan, combine soup and milk; heat just to boil, stirring
until smooth. Pour over potato mixture in baking dish; arrange
browned chops on top. Cover dish with foil. Bake, covered, 30
minutes. Remove foil; bake 1 hour longer, or until potatoes are
tender. Makes 4 to 6 servings.

✿ *Pork Chops and Green Beans*

6 pork chops, cut ¾ inch
   thick
1 teaspoon salt
⅛ teaspoon pepper
2 (10 oz.) packages frozen
   cut green beans, thawed

1 can condensed cream of
   celery soup
½ teaspoon ground nutmeg
⅓ cup milk
¼ teaspoon salt

Heat oven to 350°. Trim excess fat from chops; use to grease a medium-size skillet. Season the chops with 1 teaspoon salt and the pepper and place in skillet. Brown lightly over moderately high heat. Mix green beans, soup, nutmeg, milk, and ¼ teaspoon salt in a shallow 2-quart baking dish. Arrange chops on top. Cover and bake 45 minutes, or until meat is fork tender. Makes 4 to 6 servings.

✿ *Pork Chops in Orange Sauce*

8 thinly sliced pork chops
1 cup water
½ cup frozen orange juice
   concentrate
½ cup dark raisins
2 tablespoons light brown
   sugar

1 teaspoon salt
½ teaspoon cinnamon
dash cloves
2 teaspoons cornstarch
1 tablespoon water
1 small orange, thinly sliced

Slowly heat large skillet. Add pork chops, 4 at a time, and brown well on both sides. When all chops are browned, pour off all fat. Arrange chops, overlapping slightly, in skillet. Add 1 cup water, orange juice, and raisins; sprinkle with brown sugar, salt, cinnamon, and cloves. Simmer, covered, 30 to 40 minutes, or until chops are tender. Remove chops to platter; keep warm. Pour pan juices into 2-cup measure; if necessary, add water to make 1¼ cups. Return to skillet; bring to boil. Mix cornstarch with 1 tablespoon water; stir into boiling liquid. Add sliced orange. Reduce heat and simmer 3 minutes, stirring several times. Spoon over chops. Makes 4 servings.

❀ *Pork Pie*

1½ cups diced potato
boiling salted water
1 cup diced carrots
¼ cup thinly sliced celery
1 (8 oz.) can boiled onions,
  drained
2 cups ½-inch cubes
  leftover cooked pork

1 (10½ oz.) can mushroom
  gravy
¼ teaspoon paprika
½ teaspoon salt
1 stick pie crust mix (or
  enough pastry for 9-inch
  pie crust)

Cook potatoes in boiling salted water for 5 minutes; add carrots and continue cooking 5 minutes; add celery and cook 10 minutes (total cooking time of 20 minutes). Drain vegetables. Heat oven to 450°. Combine cooked vegetables, onions, pork, gravy, paprika, and salt. Pour into a shallow 1½-quart baking dish. Prepare pastry according to package directions. Roll out to fit top of baking dish. Place over meat mixture and flute edge; make a few slits in top. Bake 20 to 25 minutes, or until crust is browned. Makes 4 servings.

❀ *Saucy Baked Ribs*

4 pounds spareribs
salt
pepper
1 (8 oz.) can tomato sauce
¼ cup brown sugar
¼ cup light corn syrup or
  molasses
¼ cup chopped onion

1 clove garlic, minced
1 apple, peeled and diced
2 tablespoons raisins
1 tablespoon vinegar
½ teaspoon prepared
  mustard
½ teaspoon Worcestershire
  sauce

Cut spareribs in serving pieces and place in shallow baking pan. Bake at 350° for 1 hour. Meanwhile, combine remaining ingredients; simmer for 15 minutes. Remove excess fat from spareribs; cover ribs with sauce. Bake spareribs 40 minutes longer, basting occasionally. Makes 4 to 5 servings.

❀ *Smoked Pork Shoulder with Kidney Beans*

1 pound dried red kidney
    beans
water
2½ pounds smoked pork
    shoulder
2 teaspoons salt
¼ teaspoon pepper

1 bay leaf
¼ cup chopped celery
½ cup chopped onion
1 quart water
1 small head cabbage,
    coarsely shredded

Wash beans carefully. Place in large, heavy saucepan or Dutch oven. Add water just to cover beans. Place over moderate heat and bring to boil. Cook 2 minutes. Remove pan from heat and let beans stand 1 hour. Add the pork shoulder (leave casing on so meat will stay together), salt, pepper, bay leaf, celery, onion, and 1 quart water to beans. Place over moderate heat and bring to boil. Cover tightly; reduce heat to low and simmer 1 hour. Add shredded cabbage and continue to simmer 30 minutes. To serve: remove meat to cutting board, peel off outside casing, and cut in thin slices. Season beans and cabbage with more salt, if necessary, and serve with sliced meat. Makes 6 servings.

❀ *Spareribs and Sauerkraut Baked in Cider*

2 racks spareribs, with
    center bones cracked
    (about 3 lbs.)
1 teaspoon salt
¼ teaspoon pepper
1 pound sauerkraut,
    drained

1 cup pared, thinly sliced
    apples
1 teaspoon caraway seed
2 cups apple cider
1 tablespoon light brown
    sugar

Preheat oven to 350°. Wipe ribs with damp paper towels; sprinkle with salt and pepper. Place ribs, fat side down, on rack in shallow roasting pan. Bake, uncovered, 30 minutes. Pour off drippings. Turn ribs; bake 20 minutes longer. On one rack of spareribs, spread drained sauerkraut; then layer with apple slices and sprinkle with caraway seed. Pour over ¾ cup cider. Cover with second rack of ribs; fasten with skewers. Cover pan loosely with foil. Bake 1½ hours, basting several times with ¾ cup of remaining cider. Uncover pan. Baste with rest of cider. Sprinkle top of ribs with sugar. Bake, uncovered, 30 minutes, or until nicely browned, basting occasionally with pan juices. To serve, remove to heated platter. With kitchen shears cut crosswise through both rib sections into serving pieces. Makes 3 to 4 servings.

❀ Spicy Pork Roll

1 cottage roll (2½ lbs.)
cold water
whole cloves
1 (8 oz.) can tomato sauce

⅓ cup crunchy peanut
   butter
½ teaspoon onion powder

Cover meat with cold water. Bring to boil, lower heat, and simmer 1 hour. Drain meat and place in baking dish; stud with cloves. Combine remaining ingredients; spread over meat. Bake at 325° for 30 minutes, basting occasionally with sauce. Makes 4 to 5 servings.

❀ Stove-Top Pork 'n Beans

1 pound (2 cups) small
   white dry beans
5 cups water
1 (6 oz.) can tomato paste
1 tablespoon dark corn
   syrup or molasses

2 teaspoons salt
1 bay leaf
1 onion, quartered
2 fresh pig hocks (about 1
   lb.)

Wash beans and place in large kettle with 4 cups water. Bring to boil. Cover, set aside for 2 hours. Combine remaining cup water with tomato paste, corn syrup, salt, bay leaf. Stir into undrained beans. Add onion and pig hocks (unskinned but washed). Bring to boil, cover. Simmer about 2 hours, until pork and beans are tender. Remove skin and bones from hocks, leaving meat with beans. Makes 4 servings.

❀ Stuffed Pork Shoulder

1 pound dried prunes
1 cup dry sherry
5 to 6 pounds fresh pork
   shoulder

2 tablespoons flour
1 cup milk
salt
pepper

Wash prunes; drain thoroughly. Add sherry and let stand in re-

frigerator overnight. Remove pits from prunes. Have the butcher
remove bone from pork shoulder, leaving a pocket for prunes. Pack
prunes into meat. Bring edges of opening together and fasten with
metal skewers. Heat oven to 325°. Place meat on rack in shallow
baking pan. Bake, uncovered, 35 to 40 minutes per pound, or about
3½ hours. After meat has cooked 1 hour, remove from oven and peel
off hard rind. Return to oven and continue cooking. When pork is
cooked, remove to serving platter. Skim off most of the fat from
the pan juices. Add flour to juices and mix well. Gradually add milk;
cook and stir over moderate heat until thickened. Season with salt
and pepper; serve with pork. Makes 8 servings.

❀ *Tangy Brown Ribs*

2 pounds meaty pork ribs
salt
pepper
1 onion, chopped
2 tablespoons vinegar

2 tablespoons brown sugar
1 teaspoon prepared
   mustard
2 (8 oz.) cans or 1 (15 oz.)
   can tomato sauce

Place meat in baking dish; sprinkle with salt and pepper. Bake 45
minutes at 375°. Drain fat. Combine onion, vinegar, sugar, and
mustard; spread on meat. Pour tomato sauce over all. Bake at 350°
for 30 minutes, or until done, basting occasionally with sauce. Makes
6 servings.

HAMBURGER

Hamburger has a lot going for it.

It has speed and ease of cooking; it is nutritious and cheap. It is also versatile. It doesn't *have* to be trapped in a roll and bathed in mustard or ketchup. In fact, there are more variations on basic hamburger recipes than computers have dreamed of. A writer preparing a cookbook of different ways to serve hamburger every day of the year didn't run out of recipes—she ran out of days!

There is no question that hamburger is the salvation of home-makers struggling to get through this week's meals without spending next week's budget. In general, stores feature four kinds of ground beef: regular ground beef which has the highest fat content (as much as 30 percent) and is usually ground from flank, brisket, shanks, neck meat, etc., ground chuck (10 to 20 percent fat), ground round (about 10 percent fat), and ground sirloin (less than 10 percent fat).

Good ground beef should contain no more than 12 to 25 percent fat. You can usually tell how much fat filler has been included by the appearance of the meat. A light pink color with lots of white flecks means the fat content is high and that you are going to wind up with 50 percent grease for your drippings can and 50 percent meat left to serve the family. However, don't think that hamburger without some fat ground into it is the ideal. Fat gives flavor to hamburger; without it, the meat can be dry and tasteless. If, perchance, you buy hamburger ground from lean flank steak, it is smart to add two to four tablespoons of fat per pound just to give the meat a juicier taste. Hamburger should be red in color, slightly flecked with white, and preferably medium-coarse ground. Ground too fine, it will lose flavor.

It is important to choose the right kind of ground meat for the dish you are planning. If you are going to grill or pan-broil patties, select chuck or round; these have enough fat content for self-basting to keep the patties moist and juicy, but not so much fat as to cause excessive shrinkage.

If you are preparing a ground beef casserole where fat will not be drained off during the cooking, you should pick the very leanest ground beef. If you are browning the meat and draining off the fat before adding other ingredients, choose regular ground beef.

Markets frequently have specials on ground beef. Since hamburger is one meat that can be frozen successfully, stock up on these specials. Shape the meat into patties and wrap separately in foil or plastic and freeze. Always make your own hamburger patties; you pay pennies more for those ready-shaped patties at the meat counter. If you're going to use the meat in recipes like spaghetti sauce or chili, brown it first and freeze the crumbled, cooked meat. In either case, do not add any seasonings until you are ready to do the final cooking. Freezing has a tendency to increase their potency.

Freshness is vital in hamburger; the meat will keep its flavor and freshness two or three days if stored in a tightly covered glass, porcelain, or plastic dish in the coldest spot in the refrigerator.

Incidentally, you can stretch hamburger to make even thriftier meals. One pound of meat will stretch to six servings when you add either a cup of cooked rice, a slice of stale bread soaked in water then squeezed dry, or a cup of fine dry bread crumbs soaked in milk 20 minutes, until the milk has been absorbed. When making meatballs or meat loaves, add one egg to each pound of meat as a binding agent and a few drops of water to keep the meat moist.

❈ Around-the-World Burgers

BASIC BURGER:

1 pound lean ground beef	½ teaspoon salt
¼ cup fine bread crumbs	⅛ teaspoon pepper
¼ cup minced onion	1 (8 oz.) can tomato sauce

Combine first 5 ingredients with ¼ cup tomato sauce. Mix well. Shape into 4 large patties. Brown on both sides; pour off fat. Simmer in one of the following sauces for an "international" flavor. Makes 4 servings.

Mexican Burgers: Combine remaining tomato sauce with 1 (15½ oz.) can kidney beans, ¼ cup chopped onion, and 1 teaspoon chili powder. Pour over burgers and simmer 15 minutes. Just before serving, sprinkle burgers with shredded Cheddar cheese.

German Burgers: Combine remaining tomato sauce, ¼ cup vinegar, ⅓ cup water, 5 whole cloves, and 5 crumbled gingersnaps. Pour over hamburgers and simmer 15 minutes.

Italian Burgers: Combine remaining tomato sauce with ¼ teaspoon oregano, ¼ teaspoon basil, and ¼ cup water; pour over burgers. Top each burger with slice of Mozzarella cheese. Simmer 15 minutes.

Swedish Burgers: Combine remaining tomato sauce with ½ cup white wine, ¼ teaspoon nutmeg, and 1 tablespoon sugar. Pour over burgers and simmer 20 minutes.

Western Burgers: Combine remaining tomato sauce with 1 teaspoon Worcestershire sauce, ¼ teaspoon salt, ¼ cup water, and 1 small can sliced ripe olives. Pour over burgers and simmer 15 minutes.

❀ *Baja Burgers*

1 pound lean ground beef
½ cup crushed corn chips
salt
pepper
1 (8 oz.) can tomato sauce
  with onions
¼ teaspoon garlic salt

¼ teaspoon chili powder
4 French rolls, split and
  toasted
¼ cup diced green chilis or
  sliced stuffed olives
¼ cup shredded sharp
  Cheddar cheese

Mix beef and corn chips; shape into 4 oblong patties to fit rolls. Sprinkle with salt and pepper. In skillet cook, turning once, about 6 to 10 minutes, or until done to your liking. Combine tomato sauce, garlic salt, and chili powder; add to skillet and simmer a few minutes to blend flavors. Place burgers on roll bottoms and top with sauce, chilis, and cheese. Cover with roll tops. Makes 4 servings.

❁ Basic Meat Loaf

1 (6 oz.) can tomato paste
¾ cup water
1 teaspoon salt
¼ teaspoon basil
¼ teaspoon pepper
1½ pounds ground beef

1½ cups fresh bread
  crumbs
½ cup chopped onion
1 clove garlic, minced
1 egg

Stir together tomato paste, water, salt, basil, and pepper. Set aside. Combine beef, bread crumbs, onion, garlic, and egg with ½ cup tomato paste mixture. Shape meat mixture into loaf and place in shallow baking dish. Bake at 350° for 1 hour. Drain fat. Pour remaining tomato paste mixture over top of loaf. Bake 15 minutes longer. Makes 6 servings.

❁ Beef 'n Biscuit Pie

1 pound ground beef
  (chuck)
½ cup chopped onion
1 (8 oz.) can tomato sauce
1 teaspoon salt

1 teaspoon chili powder
⅔ cup milk
¼ cup salad oil
2 cups packaged biscuit mix

In skillet brown beef with onion; pour off fat. Add tomato sauce, salt, and chili powder; bring to boil and keep hot. Meanwhile, combine milk and salad oil and stir into biscuit mix. On lightly floured surface knead dough 8 to 10 times; divide in half. Pat one half into 9-inch pie pan; pour in hot filling. Pat out remaining dough to 10-inch circle and place over filling. Crimp edges to seal. Make slashes for steam vents in top. Bake at 425° for 20 to 25 minutes. Makes 4 servings.

❁ Beef and Lima Bake

1 package frozen Fordhook
  lima beans
2 tablespoons salad oil
1 medium onion, sliced
1 pound ground beef
  (chuck)

2 tablespoons chopped
  parsley
1 teaspoon salt
⅛ teaspoon pepper
1 can condensed tomato
  soup

Heat oven to 400°. Let package of lima beans stand at room temperature while preparing other ingredients. Heat oil in skillet over moderate heat; add onion and cook until soft. Add meat; break up with a fork. Cook and stir until meat is brown. Blend in parsley, salt, pepper, and soup. Break up beans and add to meat. Bring mixture to a boil. Turn into a greased 1½-quart casserole. Bake 20 minutes. Makes 4 servings.

❀ *Beef Porcupines*

1 pound ground beef	*¼ teaspoon pepper*
½ cup raw rice	*2 tablespoons salad oil*
¼ cup chopped onion	*2 (8 oz.) cans tomato sauce*
1 teaspoon salt	*1 cup water*

Mix beef, rice, onion, and seasonings. Form into small balls. Fry in hot salad oil, turning frequently, until light brown but not crusty on all sides. Add tomato sauce and water; mix well. Cover and simmer about 45 minutes. Makes 4 servings.

❀ *Burger-Stuffed Onions*

6 large onions	*¼ to ½ teaspoon chili*
1 pound lean ground beef	*powder*
2 tablespoons chopped	*½ teaspoon salt*
green pepper	*⅛ teaspoon pepper*
2 tablespoons dry bread	*3 slices American cheese*
crumbs	

Peel onions and cook in boiling salted water about 30 minutes. Drain and cool. Slice off top third of each onion; cut out centers to make cups. Chop ½ cup of the centers and sauté with beef and green pepper for 5 minutes. Mix in bread crumbs, chili powder, salt, and pepper. Fill onion cups with meat mixture; place onions in shallow greased baking dish. Cut each slice of cheese into 4 strips. Crisscross strips of cheese over onions. Bake at 350° for 20 minutes, or until done. Makes 6 servings.

❀ *Cheese-Beef Pinwheels*

2 tablespoons butter or
  margarine
⅔ cup finely chopped
  onion
½ teaspoon seasoned salt
1 teaspoon Worcestershire
  sauce
¾ cup shredded sharp
  Cheddar cheese
1 egg, slightly beaten

¼ cup milk
¼ teaspoon dried thyme
  leaves
1 teaspoon Worcestershire
  sauce
1 teaspoon salt
⅛ teaspoon pepper
1¼ pounds ground beef
¾ cup crushed bite-size
  shredded corn biscuits

Melt butter in skillet; add onion and cook over moderate heat until tender. Mix onion, seasoned salt, 1 teaspoon Worcestershire, and cheese; reserve cheese mixture to use as filling. Combine egg, milk, thyme, 1 teaspoon Worcestershire, and the salt and pepper. Thoroughly combine egg mixture, meat, and cereal crumbs. Heat oven to 325°. Place meat on sheet of wax paper and pat into a 6 by 10 inch rectangle. Spread the cheese filling over meat. Roll up like a jelly roll, starting at the short side, using wax paper to help lift meat. Cut crosswise into 6 slices; place in a buttered baking dish. Bake about 40 minutes. Makes 4 to 6 servings.

❀ *Chili Olé*

1 pound lean ground beef
1 onion, chopped
1 teaspoon chili powder
1 teaspoon salt
½ cup elbow macaroni
2 (8 oz.) cans tomato sauce

1 cup water
1 (1 lb.) can kidney beans,
  drained
½ cup shredded sharp
  Cheddar cheese

Brown meat in skillet. Add other ingredients except cheese. Cover and simmer 12 to 15 minutes, or until macaroni is tender. Add cheese and heat until melted. Makes 4 to 5 servings.

✤ *Eggplant and Meatballs Parmigiana*

TOMATO SAUCE:

2 tablespoons margarine
½ cup chopped onion
1 clove garlic, crushed
1 (1 lb.) can tomatoes, with liquid
1 tablespoon sugar

½ teaspoon salt
1 teaspoon dried oregano leaves
½ teaspoon dried basil leaves
¼ teaspoon pepper

EGGPLANT AND MEATBALLS:

1 large eggplant (1½ lbs.)
¼ cup flour
1 teaspoon seasoned salt
⅛ teaspoon pepper
¼ cup salad oil
1½ pounds ground beef (chuck)

½ teaspoon salt
¼ cup grated Parmesan cheese
½ (8 oz.) package Mozzarella cheese, sliced

TOMATO SAUCE: In hot margarine in medium saucepan, sauté onion and garlic until onion is golden brown—about 5 minutes. Add remaining sauce ingredients; bring to boil. Reduce heat and simmer, uncovered, 10 minutes.

Meanwhile, wash eggplant. Cut crosswise into slices ½ inch thick. Combine flour, seasoned salt, and pepper; use to coat eggplant. In 2 tablespoons hot oil in skillet, sauté eggplant slices, a few at a time. Add more oil as needed. Set aside slices as they brown. Preheat oven to 350°. Sprinkle chuck with salt; gently shape into 8 patties about ½ inch thick. Broil, 4 inches from heat, 5 minutes on each side. Spoon half of tomato sauce into a 13 by 9 by 2 inch baking dish. Arrange eggplant and meat in dish. Spoon remaining sauce on top. Sprinkle with Parmesan cheese; top with Mozzarella. Bake, uncovered, 30 minutes, or just until Mozzarella is melted and golden. Makes 8 servings.

❀ *French-Fry Pizza*

*1 (1 lb.) package frozen
  French-fried potatoes*
1 pound ground beef
½ cup chopped onion
*½ cup chopped green
  pepper*
1 clove garlic, minced
*1 (8 oz.) can tomato sauce
  with cheese*

*1 tablespoon
  Worcestershire sauce*
*1 (4 oz.) can sliced ripe
  olives*
½ teaspoon oregano
½ teaspoon basil
½ teaspoon salt
*½ pound Mozzarella
  cheese, cut in strips*

Stand shortest French fries close together around edge of 9-inch pie pan; break up remaining French fries and cover bottom of pan. Bake as package directs until browned. Meanwhile, in skillet lightly brown ground beef; pour off fat. Add onion, green pepper, and garlic; cook until almost tender. Add tomato sauce, Worcestershire, olives, oregano, basil, and salt; simmer 10 minutes. Carefully pour over French fries. Garnish with cheese. Bake at 450° for 10 minutes. Makes 6 servings.

❀ *Go-Go Goulash*

2 slices bacon, diced
*1½ pounds lean ground
  beef*
1½ teaspoons salt
1 medium onion, sliced
*2 (8 oz.) cans or 1 (15 oz.)
  can tomato sauce with
  tomato bits*
*1 (12 oz.) can whole kernel
  corn*

1 cup water
*1 green pepper, coarsely
  chopped*
1 cup thickly sliced celery
*½ cup elbow or shell
  macaroni*
2 teaspoons chili powder
¼ teaspoon garlic powder

In Dutch oven or large, heavy saucepan cook bacon until almost crisp. Meanwhile, combine beef and ½ teaspoon salt; shape into 1-inch balls. Brown meatballs in bacon drippings. Add onion; cook until golden. Pour off fat. Add 1 teaspoon salt and remaining ingredients. Bring to boil, reduce heat, and simmer 35 to 45 minutes, stirring occasionally to prevent macaroni from sticking. Skim off any fat. Makes 6 to 8 servings.

❀ *Hamburger Balls with Onion Sauce*

1 tablespoon instant minced onion
1 tablespoon water
1 pound lean ground beef
1 tablespoon chopped parsley
1 egg
½ teaspoon salt
1 tablespoon salad oil

3 tablespoons butter or margarine
5 medium onions, thinly sliced
¼ pound mushrooms, thinly sliced
½ teaspoon salt
1 cup canned beef consommé

Sprinkle onion over water and let stand 5 minutes to hydrate. Mix together meat, onion, parsley, egg, and ½ teaspoon salt. Shape heaping tablespoonfuls of meat into balls. There should be about 15 balls. Heat oil in skillet over moderately high heat; brown meatballs on all sides. Remove balls from skillet. Melt butter in skillet over moderately low heat; add onions and cook until golden brown. Add mushrooms, ½ teaspoon salt, and beef consommé; mix together. Add browned meatballs; cover and heat over moderately low heat for 20 minutes. Makes 4 servings.

❀ *Hamburger Stroganoff*

1 pound lean ground beef
1 medium onion, chopped
1 clove garlic, minced
1 teaspoon salt
¼ teaspoon pepper
2 tablespoons flour

1 (8 oz.) can tomato sauce with mushrooms
1 cup commercial sour cream
hot cooked noodles or rice

In large skillet brown beef and onion. Add garlic, salt, and pepper; stir in flour. Pour in tomato sauce and simmer 5 minutes. Stir in sour cream and heat a few minutes. Serve over noodles or rice. Makes 4 to 5 servings.

✿ *Hash Florentine*

3 to 4 cups ground or finely
    chopped cooked beef
1 large potato, finely
    chopped
1 onion, finely chopped
2 tablespoons salad oil
1 (8 oz.) can tomato sauce
    with cheese
2 teaspoons Worcestershire
    sauce

1 teaspoon salt
¼ teaspoon pepper
2 (10 oz.) packages frozen
    chopped spinach, cooked
6 eggs
salt
pepper

Sauté beef, potato, and onion in salad oil in skillet until lightly
browned. Add ½ can tomato sauce, Worcestershire, salt, and pepper;
combine well. Place 6 mounds of spinach on top of hash; make
depressions in the mounds with back of spoon. Break eggs into depressions; sprinkle with salt and pepper. Cover and cook until eggs
are almost done. Pour on remaining ½ can tomato sauce. Cover and
cook until eggs are done. Makes 6 servings.

✿ *Meat Loaf in Pastry*

1½ pounds ground beef
    (chuck)
½ cup finely chopped
    celery
½ cup finely chopped
    onion
1½ cups fine dry bread
    crumbs

2 eggs, well beaten
⅔ cup finely cubed sharp
    American cheese
1 teaspoon garlic salt
1 teaspoon salt
¼ teaspoon pepper
1 package pastry mix
1 egg, slightly beaten

Heat oven to 375°. Combine beef, celery, onion, bread crumbs, the
2 eggs, cheese, garlic salt, salt, and pepper. Toss to blend thoroughly. Shape into a loaf about 8 by 4 by 2 inches. Place in a flat
baking pan or loaf pan. Bake 45 minutes. Remove loaf from pan;
cool 15 minutes. Heat oven to 425°. Prepare pastry as directed on
package. Roll out on lightly floured board into rectangle about ⅛
inch thick and large enough to fit completely around meat loaf.
Gently wrap pastry around loaf so edges meet on one side near
bottom. Carefully seal the seam. Fold in ends and pinch to seal.

Brush with beaten egg. Bake 15 to 20 minutes, until pastry is golden brown. Cut in slices to serve. Makes 6 servings.

✿ *Meatball Minestrone*

1 pound lean ground beef
1 egg
¼ cup cracker crumbs
¼ cup finely chopped onion
1 teaspoon salt
¼ teaspoon pepper
2 (8 oz.) cans or 1 (15 oz.) can tomato sauce with tomato bits

2½ cups water
1 (15½ oz.) can red kidney beans, with liquid
1 cup sliced celery
¼ cup uncooked elbow macaroni
½ teaspoon oregano
¼ teaspoon thyme

Combine beef, egg, crumbs, onion, salt, and pepper; shape into 16 meatballs. In large saucepan brown meatballs; pour off fat. Add remaining ingredients. Bring to boil; simmer, covered, 25 to 30 minutes, or until macaroni is tender. Makes 4 generous servings.

✿ *Noodle-Beef Bake*

1 pound ground beef
½ cup chopped onion
1 cup water
1½ teaspoons salt
¼ teaspoon oregano
¼ teaspoon basil
⅛ teaspoon pepper
1 clove garlic, crushed

1 (8 oz.) package wide noodles, cooked and drained
1½ cups cottage cheese
½ cup shredded Mozzarella or process American cheese

In skillet brown beef with onion; pour off fat. Stir in water, 1 teaspoon salt, oregano, basil, pepper, and garlic; simmer 5 to 10 minutes. Gently mix cooked noodles, cottage cheese, and ½ teaspoon salt. In 2-quart baking dish alternate layers of noodles and meat sauce, beginning with noodles and ending with meat sauce. Sprinkle with Mozzarella. Bake at 350° for 25 to 30 minutes. Makes 6 servings.

❀ *Peanut Meatballs*

1 pound lean ground beef
⅓ cup coarsely chopped
  salted peanuts
1 small onion, minced
½ teaspoon salt

⅛ teaspoon pepper
1 egg, slightly beaten
1 cup water
1 teaspoon steak sauce
1½ teaspoons brown sugar

Combine beef with peanuts, onion, salt, pepper, and egg. Form into 12 to 15 balls. Brown on all sides in heavy skillet. Mix water with steak sauce and sugar. Pour over meatballs. Cover and simmer 20 minutes. Makes 4 to 6 servings.

❀ *Polynesian Beef Skillet*

½ pound ground beef
  (chuck)
½ teaspoon meat tenderizer
1½ teaspoons curry powder
¼ teaspoon salt
1 tablespoon salad oil
½ cup sliced onion
½ green pepper, thinly
  sliced

¼ cup seedless raisins
¼ cup chopped salted
  peanuts
1 bay leaf
⅓ cup water
⅓ cup raw rice, cooked
  according to package
  directions

Mix ground beef, meat tenderizer, curry, and salt. Heat salad oil in skillet; add onion and green pepper and cook over moderate heat until tender. Add ground beef mixture and cook and stir until lightly browned. Add raisins, nuts, bay leaf, and water. Cover and simmer 20 minutes, stirring occasionally. Serve meat over hot cooked rice. Makes 2 servings.

❀ *Saturday Meat Loaf*

1½ pounds lean ground beef
½ cup fresh bread crumbs
2 eggs
½ cup chopped onion
1 teaspoon salt

¼ teaspoon pepper
2 (8 oz.) cans or 1 (15 oz.)
  can tomato sauce with
  tomato bits

Combine beef, bread crumbs, eggs, onion, salt, and pepper with

⅓ cup of the tomato sauce. In shallow baking pan shape into loaf. Bake at 350° for 1 hour; pour off fat. Pour remaining tomato sauce over loaf. Bake 10 minutes more. Makes 6 servings.

✿ Spinach Meat Loaf with Tomato Sauce

3 pounds fresh spinach
2 pounds ground beef
  (chuck)
1½ cups cold cooked rice
1 cup finely chopped onion
¾ teaspoon nutmeg

¼ teaspoon cinnamon
3 teaspoons salt
few grains pepper
3 eggs, slightly beaten
4 slices bacon
Tomato Sauce

Wash spinach well in several changes of water. Drain. Place in a kettle or large saucepan and cook over moderately low heat 12 to 15 minutes, or until tender. Heat oven to 350°. Drain spinach thoroughly and chop finely; place on paper towels to absorb excess moisture. Mix together spinach, meat, rice, onion, nutmeg, cinnamon, salt, and pepper. Stir in eggs. Pack into 2 buttered 8½ by 4½ by 2¾ inch loaf pans. Place 2 slices of bacon on top of each loaf. Bake 50 to 60 minutes, until firm. Let stand a few minutes, then remove to warm platter. Spoon Tomato Sauce over each loaf and serve. Makes 8 servings.

TOMATO SAUCE: Cook 1 cup chopped onion and 2 cloves minced garlic in 2 tablespoons salad oil until soft. Add 2 (6 oz.) cans tomato paste, 3 cups water, 2 teaspoons salt, 1 teaspoon sugar, 1 teaspoon oregano, ¼ teaspoon pepper, and a bay leaf. Simmer, uncovered, 30 minutes. Remove bay leaf. Makes 4 cups. Use half for Spinach Meat Loaf; freeze half for later use.

✿ Stuffed Cabbage

1 large head cabbage
2 pounds ground beef
  (chuck)
¾ cup raw rice
2 eggs

1 large onion, finely
  chopped
½ teaspoon salt
½ cup vinegar
½ cup brown sugar
water

Drop whole cabbage into boiling water in a large saucepan. Let stand about 5 minutes, until soft enough to separate the leaves.

Drain and cool enough to handle. Cut out hard stem end and carefully remove leaves, being sure to keep them as whole as possible. Combine beef, rice, eggs, onion, and salt; blend thoroughly. Place a tablespoonful of the mixture in the center of each cabbage leaf; roll leaf around meat and tuck in the ends. Place rolls close together in a large saucepan. Combine vinegar and sugar; add water to make just enough sauce to cover the rolls. Cover tightly; simmer over low heat 1 hour. Remove cover and cook about 15 minutes, until sauce is slightly thickened. Makes 8 servings.

❀ Stuffed Green Peppers

6 *medium green peppers*
1 *pound lean ground beef*
2 *cups cooked rice*
¼ *cup chopped onion*
1½ *teaspoons salt*

⅛ *teaspoon pepper*
2 *(8 oz.) cans or 1 (15 oz.)*
  can tomato sauce with
  tomato bits
1 *cup shredded cheese*

Wash and halve green peppers lengthwise; remove seeds. Lightly mix beef, rice, onion, salt, pepper, and ½ cup tomato sauce. Pile into pepper halves, top with cheese; arrange in shallow baking dish. Pour remaining tomato sauce over peppers. Cover and bake at 350° for 1 hour. Makes 6 servings.

❀ Sweet and Sour Meatballs

½ *pound ground beef*
  (chuck)
2 *tablespoons fine dry bread*
  crumbs
2 *tablespoons milk*
2 *tablespoons chopped*
  onion
½ *teaspoon salt*
few grains pepper

1 *tablespoon butter or*
  margarine
½ *cup water*
1 *teaspoon vinegar*
2 *tablespoons ketchup*
1 *tablespoon dark corn*
  syrup
¼ *teaspoon basil*
¼ *teaspoon salt*
3 *gingersnaps, crumbled*

Mix ground beef, bread crumbs, milk, onion, ½ teaspoon salt, and pepper. Shape into 6 balls. Melt butter in skillet; add meat balls and brown lightly on all sides. Mix water, vinegar, ketchup, corn syrup, basil, and ¼ teaspoon salt; pour over meat balls. Add gingersnap crumbs; cover and cook 20 minutes. Makes 2 servings.

✸ Tamale Pie Oliva

1½ pounds ground beef
1 onion, chopped
1 clove garlic, minced
1 (14½ oz.) can whole
   tomatoes
1 (1 lb.) can whole kernel
   corn, drained
2 to 3 teaspoons chili
   powder

2 teaspoons salt
1 (4½ oz.) can sliced ripe
   olives
1 cup corn meal
1 cup milk
2 eggs, well beaten
1½ cups grated American
   cheese

Brown beef in skillet; add onion and garlic and cook until tender. Drain excess fat. Add tomatoes, corn, and seasonings, cover and simmer 15 minutes. Pour into 8 by 12 by 2 inch pan. Top with sliced olives. Mix corn meal, milk, and eggs; spread over filling. Sprinkle with cheese. Bake at 350° for 45 minutes. Makes 8 to 10 servings.

✸ Texas Hash

1 pound ground beef
1 onion, chopped
1 green pepper, chopped
2 (14½ oz.) cans whole
   tomatoes

1 teaspoon chili powder
1½ teaspoons salt
1 teaspoon Worcestershire
   sauce
¾ cup raw regular rice

Brown beef in skillet. Add onion and green pepper and cook until tender. Drain fat. Add tomatoes and seasonings; bring to a boil. Stir in rice. Cover and simmer 30 to 35 minutes. Makes 4 to 6 servings.

FRANKFURTERS AND SAUSAGE

Frankfurters, franks, hot dogs, wieners—call them what you will but recognize them as economical, easy ways to feed the family and stay within your food budget. Like hamburgers they have a universal appeal, especially among the small fry. And like hamburgers, they don't have to be clamped in a roll and laced with ketchup, mustard, or relish; there are other, more imaginative ways to serve them.

When you shop for frankfurters make certain to read the label on the package. Some are all meat; others are not. Those containing cereals or dried milk are perfectly good, but you should not pay all-meat prices for them.

Actually, frankfurters are part of the sausage clan. Other members of the same family tree include knockwurst (flavored with garlic), Viennawurst (tiny franks cut at either end), and kielbasa, a Polish sausage highly flavored with garlic and other seasonings. Since they have all been cooked and/or smoked in their preparation, they needn't be cooked at home. However, they taste best when heated by simmering in water to cover, split and broiled, or baked in casserole dishes.

Frankfurters are frequently supermarket weekend "loss leaders," or attractions to get customers to a store. Don't judge these specials by the packer's name alone. Remember that the company name may not tell the whole story. Each packer has several different brand names to denote the different qualities. You are getting good value only when the weekend special is a top-brand line at or below the price of lesser grades.

The most common fresh sausages, which must be cooked thoroughly, are all-pork sausage, country sausage, and Bockwurst. All-pork sausage comes in links, patties, or bulk and is seasoned with spices and herbs. Country sausage (also called smoked fresh sausage) often contains some ground beef or veal as well as coarsely ground pork. The chubby white sausages flecked with specks of green and known as Bockwurst are spring-time favorites. They contain beef, veal, and pork mixed with eggs, milk, seasonings, chives, and parsley, which account for those green specks. Highly perishable, they should be cooked soon after purchasing.

No sausage lesson would be complete without mentioning dry or summer sausages. Cured and sometimes smoked, they include salami, cervelat, mortadella, and pepperoni. The latter two, both Italian in origin, are highly seasoned and add zest to spaghetti and other pasta dishes.

If you are looking for an easy, hearty meal consider pork sausage for dinner as well as for breakfast. Bulk sausage is usually the thriftiest buy. Because of preparation time and labor, patties are priced about 10 cents higher per pound and links about 20 cents higher.

❀ *Baked Beans with Onion-Stuffed Franks*

2 (1 lb.) cans baked beans   *1 (4 oz.) package frozen*
1 pound frankfurters   *French-fried onion rings*
chili sauce   *salad oil*

Empty beans into shallow 1½-quart casserole. Cover and bake in a hot (450°) oven 10 minutes. Meanwhile, make a lengthwise slit in each frankfurter; spread cut surfaces with about 1 teaspoon chili sauce. Stuff frozen onion rings into slits. Arrange frankfurters on beans; brush frankfurters lightly with oil. Return to oven and bake, uncovered, 10 to 15 minutes, or until onions are slightly brown and crisp. Makes 6 to 8 servings.

🌸 *Chinatown Franks*

1 green pepper, cut in
    1-inch squares
1 medium onion, chopped
¼ cup salad oil
1 pound frankfurters, cut
    diagonally in 1-inch pieces

2 (8 oz.) cans tomato sauce
¾ cup water
2 tablespoons vinegar
2 tablespoons brown sugar
hot cooked rice

In skillet cook green pepper and onion in salad oil at medium heat until tender. Add frankfurters; brown lightly. Add tomato sauce, water, vinegar, and brown sugar; simmer 20 to 25 minutes, stirring occasionally. Serve over rice. Makes 6 servings.

🌸 *Frank-a-Roni*

1 (7¼ oz.) package
    macaroni and cheese
    dinner
1 (8 oz.) can tomato sauce
    with mushrooms
2 slices bacon, cooked and
    crumbled
3 tablespoons minced onion

2 tablespoons minced green
    pepper
1 (10 oz.) package frozen
    mixed vegetables or peas,
    thawed
½ pound frankfurters, split
    lengthwise, then cut cross-
    wise in half

Prepare macaroni-cheese dinner as label directs. Stir in tomato sauce, bacon, onion, green pepper, and mixed vegetables. Place in 1½-quart casserole. Stand frankfurters around edge of casserole. Bake at 350° for 30 minutes. Makes 4 servings.

🌸 *Frank 'n Apple Scallop*

2 large apples (about 1½
    lbs.)
2 teaspoons lemon juice
1 pound frankfurters
3 tablespoons butter or
    margarine

2 medium onions, sliced ¼
    inch thick (1 cup)
1 (6 oz.) can apple juice
3 tablespoons brown sugar,
    firmly packed
½ teaspoon salt

Core apples but do not peel; cut into ¼-inch-thick wedges. Sprinkle with lemon juice. Cut each frankfurter on the diagonal into thirds. In hot butter in large skillet sauté onion slices until golden and tender—about 5 minutes. Add apple wedges, frankfurters, apple juice, brown sugar, and salt; stir gently. Simmer, covered, about 15 minutes, or until frankfurters are puffed and apple is tender. Arrange on heated platter. Good served with potato pancakes. Makes 4 to 6 servings.

✸ Frank and Potato Casserole

1½ pounds small white
  potatoes
4 slices bacon, cut up
½ pound frankfurters, cut
  into 1-inch pieces
½ cup chopped onion
2 teaspoons flour
1 teaspoon salt

1 teaspoon sugar
¼ teaspoon celery seed
1 tablespoon vinegar
2 (8 oz.) cans tomato sauce
½ cup Cheddar cheese
  chunks
2 tablespoons minced green
  pepper or green onions

Cook unpeeled potatoes until just tender but firm. Drain and peel. Sauté bacon in skillet until crisp. Drain and save for garnish. Pour off about half of drippings. Add frankfurters and onion; cook until brown. Combine flour, salt, sugar, celery seed, vinegar, and tomato sauce and pour over frankfurters. Stir until well blended. Cube potatoes and place in shallow 2½-quart baking dish. Cover with tomato sauce mixture and garnish with Cheddar cheese chunks and bacon. Bake in 325° oven for 15 minutes. Sprinkle with minced green pepper or green onions. Makes 4 to 5 servings.

✸ Frank-Sauerkraut Casserole

1 small onion, chopped
2 tablespoons salad oil
1 (1 lb.) can sauerkraut,
  well drained
1 pound frankfurters, cut in
  1-inch pieces

1 apple, pared, cored, and
  sliced
1 cup applesauce

Sauté onion in salad oil until golden. Mix with sauerkraut. Place half of frankfurters in bottom of 1½-quart casserole. Arrange sauerkraut over frankfurters and place remaining frankfurters on top. Place apple slices on frankfurters. Pour applesauce over frankfurters. Bake at 350° for 30 minutes. Makes 4 to 5 servings.

❀ Frankfurter Supper Bake

8 slices dry bread, cubed
1 cup chopped celery
1 (8 oz.) can tomato sauce
  with onions
2 eggs, slightly beaten

2 tablespoons finely
  chopped parsley
salt and pepper to taste
1 pound frankfurters

Combine all ingredients except frankfurters. Place half the stuffing in greased 1½-quart baking dish; top with half the frankfurters. Repeat layers. Bake at 350° for 45 minutes. Makes 4 to 6 servings.

❀ Frankfurters with Vegetable Dressing

2 medium carrots, scraped
2 medium onions, peeled
2 large stalks celery, cut up
4 sprigs parsley
1½ cups chopped cooked
  spinach
1 cup soft bread crumbs
1 teaspoon salt

⅛ teaspoon pepper
1 egg, well beaten
½ cup milk
2 tablespoons bacon fat or
  salad oil
8 to 10 frankfurters, scored
  diagonally
2 slices bacon, cut in half

Grind carrots, onions, celery, and parsley, using finest blade of meat grinder. Add spinach, bread crumbs, salt, and pepper to ground vegetables. Combine egg, milk, and bacon fat; mix thoroughly with vegetables. Turn into a 12 by 7½ by 2 inch baking dish. Arrange frankfurters in single layer on top. Place bacon pieces over frankfurters. Bake about 30 minutes. Makes 4 to 6 servings.

❀ Franks in a Coat

salad oil or shortening for
  deep frying
1 cup bottled barbecue
  sauce
1 cup packaged pancake
  mix

2 tablespoons corn meal
1 tablespoon sugar
⅔ cup water
8 frankfurters

Slowly heat oil (at least 1 inch deep) in electric skillet or deep-fat fryer to 375° on deep-frying thermometer. Gently heat barbecue sauce in small saucepan. Meanwhile, combine pancake mix, corn meal, sugar, and ⅔ cup water. Beat with rotary beater until just smooth; let batter stand about 10 minutes to thicken. Dip frankfurters into batter to coat lightly all over. In hot oil fry frankfurters, a few at a time, 2 to 3 minutes, or until they are crisp and golden-brown all over. Lift out with slotted spoon and drain well on paper towels. If desired, insert wooden skewer into end of each frankfurter. Serve at once, with the hot barbecue sauce for dipping. Makes 4 servings.

❀ French Frank Fry

1 medium onion, thinly sliced

1 pound frankfurters, sliced diagonally

3 tablespoons butter or margarine

2 (9 oz.) packages frozen French-fried potatoes

2 teaspoons salt

¼ teaspoon pepper

2 (8 oz.) cans tomato sauce

½ cup Cheddar cheese chunks

2 tablespoons chopped parsley

In a large skillet, lightly sauté onion and franks in butter; push to edge of skillet, forming a ring. Place frozen French-fried potatoes in center of ring and sauté 5 minutes more, turning potatoes to brown all sides. Add salt and pepper, tomato sauce, and cheese chunks. Sprinkle with parsley. Simmer until cheese melts. Makes 4 to 5 servings.

❀ Hound Dogs

1 pound frankfurters

1 (8 oz.) can tomato sauce

4 servings mashed potatoes, instant or homemade

10 strips sliced processed cheese

Slit franks lengthwise to make pocket; spoon 1 teaspoon tomato sauce in each. Place franks ¼ inch apart in 13 by 9 by 2 inch baking dish; pat mashed potatoes down in center. Top with cheese strips. Bake at 375° 30 minutes; pour over rest of tomato sauce; bake 5 minutes more. Makes 4 servings.

❀ Kidney Bean Casserole with Hot Dogs

2 tablespoons butter or
  margarine
1 pound frankfurters, cut in
  1-inch pieces
1 clove garlic, crushed
1 cup sliced onion
2 teaspoons chili powder
¼ cup dry red wine
2 (1 lb. 1 oz.) cans kidney
  beans

¼ cup sliced celery
1 tablespoon chopped
  parsley
¾ teaspoon salt
3 tablespoons light brown
  sugar
chopped parsley

Preheat oven to 350°. In hot butter in medium skillet cook frankfurters, garlic, onion, chili powder, and wine 5 minutes. Turn mixture into 2-quart casserole. Drain 1 can beans well. Add drained beans to casserole along with undrained beans, celery, 1 tablespoon parsley, salt, and sugar; mix well. Bake, covered, 30 minutes, or until mixture is bubbly. Sprinkle with parsley. Makes 4 to 6 servings.

❀ Saturday Night Bean Bake

2 tablespoons salad oil
½ cup chopped onion
½ cup chopped celery
2 (1 lb.) cans pork and
  beans with tomato sauce
1 (1 lb.) can tomatoes, with
  liquid

1 teaspoon Italian seasoning
1 pound frankfurters (8)
1 cup grated Cheddar
  cheese

Preheat oven to 350°. In hot oil in large skillet, sauté onion and celery until tender—about 5 minutes. Remove from heat. Stir in pork and beans, tomatoes, and Italian seasoning. Turn into a 2-quart casserole. Top with frankfurters. Bake, uncovered, 40 minutes. Sprinkle cheese over top; bake a few minutes longer to melt cheese. Serve at once. Makes 8 servings.

❀ *Spanish Casserole*

1 pound frankfurters, cut
   in chunks
1 onion, chopped
1 tablespoon salad oil
2 (8 oz.) cans tomato sauce
½ cup water
3 cups cooked rice
½ teaspoon salt

dash pepper
10 pitted black olives, cut in
   half
1 cup cooked green peas or
   1 cup frozen peas, thawed
½ cup grated Cheddar
   cheese

Sauté franks and onion in salad oil. Add tomato sauce and water. Simmer until well heated. Add rice, salt, pepper, olives, and peas. Turn into 1½-quart casserole; sprinkle cheese on top. Bake at 350° for 30 minutes. Makes 6 servings.

❀ *Stuffed Franks and Sauerkraut*

4 tablespoons melted butter
   or margarine
¼ cup finely chopped onion
1 (29 oz.) can sauerkraut,
   drained
1 cup canned tomatoes
½ teaspoon caraway seeds

2 cups soft bread crumbs
1 teaspoon grated onion
¼ teaspoon ground thyme
½ teaspoon salt
2 tablespoons milk
8 frankfurters
8 slices bacon

Heat oven to 375°. Heat half the butter in a saucepan; add onion and cook over low heat until tender. Add sauerkraut, tomatoes, and caraway seeds. Pour into a large, shallow baking pan. Combine crumbs, rest of butter, grated onion, thyme, salt, and milk. Slit frankfurters lengthwise, almost through. Fill each with stuffing and wrap with a slice of bacon; secure with toothpick. Arrange on top of sauerkraut. Bake 20 to 30 minutes, until very hot. Makes 4 servings.

❀ Suppertime Sausage and Franks

2 tablespoons salad oil
1 small onion, chopped
½ pound pork sausage links
  or bulk sausage
½ pound frankfurters, cut in
  chunks
1 (1 lb.) can sauerkraut,
  drained

2 tart apples, pared, cored,
  and sliced
2 large potatoes, peeled and
  sliced
1 bouillon cube, dissolved in
  1 cup boiling water

Sauté onion in salad oil. Add sausage and frankfurters and brown lightly. Remove excess fat. Place sauerkraut in bottom of 3-quart casserole. Arrange apple slices and potato slices over it. Top with onion-meat mixture and pour bouillon over all. Bake at 350° for 1 hour. Makes 4 servings.

❀ Turkish Frankfurters

4 tablespoons salad oil
1 large onion, chopped
1 medium eggplant (about
  1 lb.)
2 tablespoons flour
½ teaspoon salt
⅛ teaspoon pepper

dash of thyme
1 small clove garlic, finely
  minced
1 (16 oz.) can tomatoes
1 pound frankfurters
hot cooked rice

Heat oil in large skillet. Add onion and cook over low heat until soft. Pare eggplant and cut into 1-inch cubes. Combine flour, salt, pepper, and thyme; add to eggplant and toss to coat pieces. Add eggplant and garlic to onion; cook until lightly browned. Stir in tomatoes. Simmer gently about 15 minutes. Add frankfurters and continue to simmer 20 minutes more. Serve with rice. Serves 4 to 6.

❀ Barbecued Sausages and Lima Beans

2 cups dried lima beans	1 cup ketchup
2 teaspoons salt	1½ tablespoons prepared
1 pound sausage links	horseradish
2 tablespoons grated onion	2 teaspoons Worcestershire
⅔ cup dark corn syrup	sauce

Wash beans; turn into medium bowl. Cover with cold water. Refrigerate, covered, overnight. Next day, drain beans. In large saucepan, cover beans with 5 cups water and the salt; bring to boil. Reduce heat; simmer, covered, 1 hour, or until beans are tender. Drain. Meanwhile, preheat oven to 400°. In large skillet, sauté sausage until browned. Drain and set aside. Combine beans with onion, corn syrup, ketchup, horseradish, and Worcestershire; mix well. Turn half of bean mixture into 2-quart casserole; cover with half of sausage. Repeat with rest of beans and sausage. Bake, uncovered, 30 minutes. Serve hot. Makes 6 servings.

❀ Homespun Sausage Bake

1 pound ground pork	¼ teaspoon salt
sausage	1 (1 lb. 13 oz.) can yellow
1 cup chopped onion	hominy, drained
1 cup sliced celery	2 cups shredded Monterey
2 (8 oz.) cans tomato sauce	Jack or Mozzarella cheese
¼ teaspoon basil or oregano	

Brown sausage, onion, and celery in skillet; pour off fat. Add tomato sauce, herb, and salt; simmer 5 minutes. In 2-quart casserole or shallow baking dish layer half the hominy, half the sausage, and half the cheese. Repeat layers, leaving center of top sausage layer uncovered by cheese. Bake at 350° for 25 minutes. Makes 4 servings.

🏵 Kielbasa with Red Cabbage

½ cup light brown sugar,
  firmly packed
1 tablespoon grated orange
  peel
1 clove garlic, crushed
1½ teaspoons salt
½ teaspoon nutmeg
¼ teaspoon pepper
⅛ teaspoon ground cloves
1 head (2 lbs.) red cabbage,
  shredded (about 12 cups)

3 medium onions, sliced
3 medium cooking apples,
  pared, cored, and sliced
1 large red pepper, cut into
  thin strips
½ cup orange juice
¼ cup red wine vinegar
1 ring (2 lbs.) kielbasa

Preheat oven to 350°. In small bowl, combine brown sugar, orange
peel, garlic, salt, nutmeg, pepper, and cloves. In Dutch oven, arrange in layers half of cabbage, half of onions, and half of apples;
sprinkle with half of brown sugar mixture; add half of pepper
strips. Repeat. Pour orange juice and vinegar over top. Bake, covered, 1 hour. Make ¼-inch-deep slashes at 2-inch intervals in kielbasa. Place in Dutch oven, pressing down to partially cover with
pan juices. Bake, covered, 30 minutes. Makes 6 servings.

🏵 Sausage-Apple Casserole

1½ pounds bulk sausage
  meat
1 (16 oz.) can sliced apples,
  drained
1 (18 oz.) can vacuum-
  packed sweet potatoes,
  sliced

¼ cup brown sugar, firmly
  packed
⅛ teaspoon cinnamon

Heat oven to 375°. Shape sausage meat into 6 or 8 uniform patties.
Cook in a skillet over moderately high heat until brown on both
sides. Pour off fat as it accumulates. Arrange sliced apples and sweet
potatoes in shallow 2-quart casserole; sprinkle with sugar and cinnamon. Place browned patties on top. Cover and bake 30 minutes.
Remove cover; bake 15 minutes longer. Makes 4 to 6 servings.

❀ Sausage Supper Dish

1½ *pounds bulk sausage*	1 *teaspoon salt*
1 *cup thinly sliced celery*	¼ *teaspoon sage, if desired*
½ *cup sliced onion*	⅛ *teaspoon pepper*
2 *(8 oz.) cans tomato sauce*	1 *(8 oz.) package noodles,*
½ *cup water*	*cooked*

Crumble sausage and brown over low heat. Drain off all fat. Add celery and onion and cook until lightly browned. Mix tomato sauce, water, and seasonings and pour over sausage. Simmer 20 minutes. Serve over hot, drained noodles. Makes 6 servings.

❀ Spanish Rice Skillet Supper

1 *pound bulk pork sausage*	1 *(8 oz.) can tomato sauce*
1 *cup raw regular rice*	2 *chicken bouillon cubes*
1 *cup chopped onion*	*dissolved in 1½ cups*
½ *cup chopped green*	*boiling water*
pepper	½ *teaspoon celery salt*
1 *clove garlic, crushed*	½ *teaspoon chili powder*

Form sausage into 4 patties; brown on both sides in 10-inch skillet; set aside. Add rice, onion, green pepper, and garlic to drippings; cook, stirring, until rice is golden and vegetables soft. Add tomato sauce, chicken broth, and seasonings; cover. Simmer 30 minutes; add sausage patties after 15 minutes. Makes 4 servings.

❀ Split Pea and Sausage Casserole

1½ *cups dried split peas*	1 *pound pork sausage links*
6 *carrots, peeled and sliced*	1 *teaspoon salt*
1 *onion, chopped*	¼ *teaspoon pepper*
1 *bay leaf*	½ *teaspoon dried marjoram*
1 *quart water*	*or basil*

Combine split peas, carrots, onion, bay leaf, and water in large saucepan; bring to boil. Reduce heat; simmer for 25 minutes. Meanwhile, cook sausage links in skillet and drain. Drain peas if necessary. Add sausage and seasonings. Pour into 1½-quart casserole and bake, covered, 45 minutes at 350°. Makes 6 servings.

LUNCHEON AND OTHER CANNED MEATS

You have probably heard about the bride who wouldn't serve luncheon meat at any other time. We trust she learned the name is a total misnomer before her first wedding anniversary. Luncheon meat can be tasty and nutritious at any hour—breakfast, lunch, dinner, or snacktime. And a thrifty choice as well.

Our favorite story about luncheon meat involves an inventive friend who wagered she could make a company meal for six with a 12-ounce can of luncheon meat. What she did was to whip up a Cheddar cheese sauce, add a third of it to the finely chopped luncheon meat, then roll up that mixture in thin pancakes. The pancakes were tucked side by side in a baking dish, the remainder of the sauce poured over them, and the whole thing popped in the oven until it was heated through and browned. We forget what her prize was, but we still remember how good those luncheon meat crêpes tasted.

There are many other canned meats that lend themselves to quick and easy menu surprises. Corned beef, roast beef hash, tongue, chipped beef—all deserve a place on what food editors like to call the Emergency Shelf. It's a good name—at one time or other everyone has been confronted with unexpected guests and no food in the house. Well, there's always *something* around but nothing you'd want to show off on the best china. That's the moment when a tin of meat on the pantry shelf looks as thrilling as a motel "Vacancy" sign at 11 P.M. on a tourists' highway.

There is no need to remind you to keep the Emergency Shelf well stocked by watching for specials on your favorite brands of canned meats. If you are someone who's confronted with a great many emergencies (which could mean either that you're a great cook or that you live close to a beach, a lake, or a ski slope), better check with your supermarket manager on case-load prices. That way your "emergencies" will be less of a shock to the budget.

❀ Baked Luncheon Meat Casserole

2 (12 oz.) cans luncheon meat
prepared mustard
1 (19 oz.) can asparagus, drained
2 cups hot mashed potatoes (prepared from instant potatoes)

2 tablespoons butter or margarine
paprika

Heat oven to 350°. Cut each can of luncheon meat into 3 slices; arrange slices in bottom of shallow 2-quart baking dish. Spread mustard over luncheon meat. Arrange asparagus over meat. Top with mashed potatoes and dot with butter. Sprinkle with paprika. Bake 30 minutes, or until potatoes start to brown. Makes 4 to 6 servings.

❀ Barbecued Luncheon Meat

1 (12 oz.) can luncheon meat
1 (8 oz.) can tomato sauce
¼ cup water
2 tablespoons brown sugar

1 tablespoon finely grated onion
¼ teaspoon Worcestershire sauce

Cut meat lengthwise, not quite through, into 8 slices. Place in greased shallow baking dish. Mix tomato sauce with rest of ingredients. Pour over meat. Bake at 425° about 30 minutes, basting occasionally. If desired, heat and baste canned new potatoes along with meat. Makes 3 servings.

❀ *Beef and Peas*

1 cup packaged precooked
rice, uncooked
1 (5 oz.) jar dried beef
1 (16 oz.) can small early
peas, with liquid
1 (4 oz.) can sliced mushrooms, drained

1 (8 oz.) can small boiled
onions, with liquid
¼ teaspoon pepper
1 cup tomato juice

Heat oven to 350°. Pour rice into a greased 2½-quart casserole. Separate dried beef slices and arrange over rice. Add the peas and liquid, the mushrooms, then the onions and liquid. Sprinkle with
pepper; pour tomato juice over top. Bake 25 minutes. Makes 3 to 4
servings.

❀ *Cheesy Broiled Hashburgers*

1 (16 oz.) can corned beef
hash
1 (3 oz.) package cream
cheese, softened
1 (8 oz.) can tomato sauce
with cheese
¼ cup well-drained pickle
relish

1 teaspoon Worcestershire
sauce
½ teaspoon dry mustard
2 hamburger or hot dog
buns, halved
butter
1 tablespoon horseradish

Combine hash, cream cheese, 2 tablespoons tomato sauce, relish,
Worcestershire, and dry mustard. Toast bun halves under broiler;
spread with butter. Mound hash mixture on each half. Slip under
broiler and broil until bubbly. Meanwhile, heat together remaining tomato sauce and horseradish. Serve over hashburgers. Makes
4 servings.

❀ Chinese Skillet

2 medium green peppers
1 small sweet red pepper
1 tablespoon butter or
    margarine
1 (14 oz.) can pineapple
    chunks with syrup
2 tablespoons cornstarch

1 teaspoon soy sauce
⅓ cup vinegar
½ cup light brown sugar,
    packed
2 (12 oz.) cans luncheon
    meat

Cut green peppers in halves; remove seeds. Cut red pepper into large chunks. Melt butter in heavy skillet over moderate heat. Add peppers and pineapple chunks and syrup and heat to boil. Combine cornstarch, soy sauce, vinegar, and sugar; turn into hot mixture. Cook and stir constantly until thickened. Cut luncheon meat into slices almost through to bottom. Place meat in sauce. Cover and simmer about 15 minutes until meat is heated. Makes 4 to 6 servings.

❀ Corned Beef and Macaroni Pie

1 (12 oz.) can corned beef
½ cup chopped onion
½ teaspoon horseradish
½ teaspoon prepared
    mustard
1 egg
1 (8 oz.) can tomato sauce
    with cheese
4 ounces elbow macaroni,
    cooked (2 cups, cooked)

1 cup shredded process
    American cheese
¼ cup evaporated milk
1 teaspoon basil
½ teaspoon salt
4 thin slices process
    American cheese, cut in
    half diagonally

Combine corned beef, onion, horseradish, mustard, egg, and ½ can tomato sauce. Pat evenly and firmly over bottom and sides of 9-inch pie pan. Mix macaroni and shredded cheese and pour into meat shell. Combine remaining tomato sauce, milk, basil, and salt; pour over macaroni. Bake at 350° for 40 minutes. Garnish with cheese slices. Makes 3 to 4 servings.

❀ Corned Beef and Potato Casserole

1 (3 oz.) can chopped
    mushrooms
1 (12 oz.) can corned beef,
    cubed
1 (1 lb. 1 oz.) can red
    kidney beans, with liquid
½ cup chili sauce
2 teaspoons Worcestershire
    sauce

½ (5⅜ oz.) package instant
    mashed potatoes
½ cup milk
½ teaspoon salt
dash pepper
2 tablespoons butter or
    margarine

Drain mushrooms, reserving liquid. In medium saucepan combine mushrooms, corned beef, kidney beans, chili sauce, and Worcestershire; mix well. Bring to boil; reduce heat and simmer, covered, stirring occasionally, 5 minutes. Add water to mushroom liquid to measure 1½ cups. Prepare potatoes as package label directs, using mushroom liquid, milk, salt, pepper, and butter. Beat potato mixture with fork until light and fluffy. Turn corned beef mixture into a 1½-quart casserole. Swirl potatoes in mounds around edge. Run under broiler 3 inches from heat 8 to 10 minutes, or until potatoes are golden. Makes 3 to 4 servings.

❀ Corned Beef-Stuffed Baked Potatoes

4 large baking potatoes
½ cup margarine
⅓ cup milk
½ teaspoon salt
dash pepper
1 cup cubed cooked corned
    beef (6 oz.)

¼ cup commercial sour
    cream
¾ teaspoon prepared
    horseradish
chopped parsley

Preheat oven to 425°. Scrub potatoes; dry thoroughly; prick skins. Bake potatoes 50 to 60 minutes, or until they can be easily pierced with a fork. Cool slightly, then slash tops. Gently squeeze open; carefully scoop out potato, keeping skins intact. Mash potato well; add margarine, milk, salt, and pepper; beat until well blended. Stir in corned beef. Spoon into potato shells. Place on cookie sheet. Bake, uncovered, 10 minutes, or until heated through. Combine sour cream and horseradish; spoon over hot potatoes. Garnish with parsley. Makes 4 servings.

❋ *Corned Beef Supper Casserole*

1 can condensed cream of celery soup	1⅓ cups packaged pre-cooked rice
1¾ cups hot water	½ cup canned French-fried onion rings
1 cup cooked or canned green beans, drained	
1 (12 oz.) can corned beef, coarsely chopped	

Heat oven to 375°. Mix soup and hot water; add green beans. Pour half of the soup mixture into a 1½-quart casserole. Arrange corned beef over soup. Sprinkle beef with the uncooked rice. Pour in remaining soup mixture. Cover and bake 10 minutes. Stir mixture gently and sprinkle with onion rings. Return to oven and bake, uncovered, 30 minutes longer. Makes 3 to 4 servings.

❋ *Crisscross Hashies*

2 (15 oz.) cans corned beef hash	1 tablespoon prepared mustard
1 tablespoon salad oil	3 slices process cheese
¼ cup pickle relish	1 (8 oz.) can tomato sauce

Chill hash. Cut into 6 even slices. Brown in salad oil in skillet. Spoon relish and mustard over each slice. Cut cheese into 12 strips. Crisscross 2 cheese strips over each burger. Pour on tomato sauce. Cover; simmer 5 minutes. Makes 6 to 8 servings.

❋ *Deviled Ham Tetrazzini*

2 cups uncooked spaghetti broken into 2-inch pieces	⅔ cup milk
1½ teaspoons instant minced onion	1 cup shredded Cheddar cheese
1 can condensed cream of chicken soup	1 teaspoon Worcestershire sauce
	2 (4½ oz.) cans deviled ham

Heat oven to 350°. Cook and drain spaghetti as directed on package. Combine spaghetti and remaining ingredients in a 3-quart casserole. Stir well to blend. Bake, covered, 20 minutes. Makes 4 to 6 servings.

❈ Dicey Bean Dish

1 (12 oz.) can luncheon
    meat, diced
½ cup chopped onion
1½ tablespoons salad oil
1 (1 lb. 14 oz.) can pork
    and beans

1 (8 oz.) can tomato sauce
1 tablespoon Worcestershire
    sauce
1 teaspoon prepared
    mustard
2 tablespoons brown sugar

Cook meat and onion in salad oil until onion is golden. Mix in remaining ingredients; pour into a 1½-quart baking dish. Bake at 350°, uncovered, for 30 to 45 minutes. Makes 4 servings.

❈ Luncheon Meat à la Mode

2 tablespoons instant
    minced onion
¼ cup water
1 (12 oz.) can luncheon
    meat, finely chopped
1 cup finely chopped celery
½ cup chopped green
    pepper
½ teaspoon dry mustard
1 (16 oz.) can tart red
    cherries

2 tablespoons cornstarch
½ cup brown sugar, firmly
    packed
few grains ground cloves
3 tablespoons lemon juice
few drops red food coloring
1 (8 oz.) can refrigerated
    biscuits
1 tablespoon butter or
    margarine

Heat oven to 425°. Mix onion and water together and let stand 5 minutes. Combine luncheon meat, celery, green pepper, mustard, and onion; spread over bottom of 9-inch square cake pan. Drain cherries and reserve juice. Mix cornstarch, brown sugar, and cloves in saucepan; stir in cherry juice, lemon juice, and red food coloring. Cook over moderate heat, stirring constantly until thickened. Fold in cherries and pour sauce over meat. Open container of biscuits and arrange biscuits over cherries. Dot biscuits with butter. Bake 25 minutes. Makes 4 servings.

❀ Meat and Rice Skillet

¼ cup bottled Italian salad
  dressing
1 (12 oz.) can luncheon
  meat, diced
1 clove garlic, crushed
1 cup chopped onion
1⅔ cups water
1⅓ cups packaged
  precooked rice

1 tablespoon dried parsley
  flakes
3 tablespoons sliced stuffed
  green olives
1 (8 oz.) can tomato sauce
  with mushrooms
grated Parmesan cheese

Heat salad dressing in large skillet. Add meat and brown lightly.
Add garlic and onion and cook until tender. Add water and bring to
a boil. Stir in rice, parsley, and olives. Remove skillet from heat and
cover. Let stand about 5 minutes. Stir in tomato sauce. Return to
heat and heat to serving temperature. Sprinkle Parmesan cheese
over top. Makes 4 servings.

❀ Meat Cube Macaroni

8 ounces elbow macaroni
½ cup butter or margarine
6 tablespoons all-purpose
  flour
1½ teaspoons salt
2½ cups milk

8 ounces sharp Cheddar
  cheese
1 (12 oz.) can luncheon
  meat, cubed
6 thick slices tomato

Cook macaroni in boiling salted water as directed on package. Drain.
Melt butter in saucepan over moderately low heat; blend in flour
and salt. Add milk gradually; cook, stirring constantly, until sauce
is smooth and thickened. Measure out 1 cup of the sauce for use
later. Pour rest of sauce over cooked macaroni and mix thoroughly.
Cut half the cheese in ¼-inch cubes; fold into macaroni with the
cubed meat. Shred rest of cheese; add to the remaining 1 cup of
sauce and heat over moderately low heat until cheese melts. Pour
macaroni mixture into a 2½-quart casserole. Arrange tomato slices on
top. Pour sauce over. Heat oven to 400°. Bake, covered, for about
25 minutes; then remove cover from casserole and bake, uncovered,

for an additional 10 or 15 minutes until hot and lightly browned. Makes 4 to 6 servings.

❁ *Open-Face Heroes*

2 (*12 oz.*) *cans luncheon*   ½ *teaspoon basil*
    meat, finely chopped   ½ *teaspoon oregano*
½ *cup finely chopped onion*   ¼ *cup salad oil*
1 *clove garlic, minced*   ¼ *cup dry sherry*
2 *medium tomatoes, finely*   1 *loaf Italian bread*
    chopped

Combine luncheon meat, onion, garlic, tomatoes, and seasonings in a large bowl. Add oil and sherry; mix thoroughly. Cut Italian bread crosswise in three sections, then cut each portion in half lengthwise (makes 6 pieces). Scoop out small portion of bread to make hollow for the filling. Then spoon the filling onto each piece of bread (about ¾ cup per portion). Place rack of broiler-frypan in lower position. Broil 3 sandwiches at a time with temperature control of broiler lid at 250°, vent open. Broil 4 to 5 minutes or until sizzling hot and lightly browned. Makes 6 servings.

❁ *Peachy Luncheon Rounds*

1 (*15½ oz.*) *can corned beef*   ¼ *teaspoon pepper*
    hash   1 (*1 lb. 13 oz.*) *can peach*
½ *teaspoon salt*   *halves*

Chill can of corned beef hash. Remove both ends of can and push hash out. Slice into 4 or 5 rounds. Place in baking dish; sprinkle with salt and pepper. Drain peach halves and save ½ cup of syrup. Place peach halves on top of hash slices and pour peach liquid over all. Bake at 350° for 30 minutes, basting occasionally. Makes 4 to 5 servings.

❀ Pineapple-Glazed Luncheon Meat

1 (6 oz.) can frozen pine-
* apple juice concentrate,*
* undiluted*
½ teaspoon powdered
* ginger*

1 tablespoon soy sauce
1 tablespoon lemon juice
¾ teaspoon salt
2 (12 oz.) cans luncheon
* meat*

In small bowl, combine pineapple juice, ginger, soy sauce, lemon juice, and salt to make a basting sauce. With sharp knife score luncheon meat—make cuts on diagonal about ⅛ inch deep and 1 inch apart; repeat from opposite direction to make squares. Grill meat on barbecue grill 4 inches from coals, basting with sauce, 8 minutes on one side. Turn; grill, basting with sauce, 8 minutes on other side, or until golden brown. Makes 8 servings.

❀ Pizza Wellingtons

1½ cups packaged biscuit
* mix*
½ cup milk
2 tablespoons salad oil
1 (12 oz.) can luncheon
* meat*
1 (6 oz.) package
* Mozzarella cheese*

1 (8 oz.) can tomato sauce
* with mushrooms*
¼ teaspoon oregano
4 teaspoons sweet pickle
* relish*

Combine biscuit mix, milk, and salad oil; prepare dough as directed for biscuits on package label. Roll into 12-inch square; cut into 4 equal squares. Meanwhile, cut luncheon meat into 12 slices. Cut cheese into 8 slices the same size as luncheon meat slices; save trimmings. Combine tomato sauce and oregano. Assemble stacks: on each biscuit square place 1 slice of meat; top, in order, with 1 cheese slice, 1 tablespoon tomato sauce, another meat slice, another cheese slice, 1 teaspoon of relish, and a final meat slice. Bring up sides of dough and seal securely. Place stacks on ungreased baking sheet. Bake at 425° for 25 minutes. Garnish stacks with reserved cheese. Serve with remaining tomato sauce. Makes 4 servings.

❁ Polka Dot Bake

¼ cup chopped onion
¼ cup chopped green
  pepper
1 tablespoon salad oil
2 (8 oz.) cans tomato sauce
  with mushrooms

1 (15 oz.) can corned beef
  hash
8 eggs
salt
pepper

Sauté onion and green pepper in salad oil. Add 1½ cans tomato sauce and simmer 5 minutes. Combine remainder of sauce with hash and pack in oiled 9 by 9 inch baking dish. Make 8 hollows in hash. Drop egg in each. Sprinkle with salt and pepper. Pour sauce over and around eggs. Bake at 350° for 15 minutes. Makes 4 to 5 servings.

❁ Sauerkraut Hash

1 (1 lb. 13 oz.) can sauerkraut, drained very
  thoroughly
2 (1 lb. 13 oz.) cans
  corned beef hash

2 tablespoons chopped
  onion
1½ teaspoons prepared
  horseradish

Place sauerkraut in bottom of greased baking dish. Combine hash, onion, and horseradish; spread over sauerkraut. Bake at 400° for 20 minutes. Makes 6 servings.

❁ Spinach Hash Pie

2 teaspoons instant minced
  onion
¼ cup milk
1 (1 lb.) can corned beef
  hash
1 (1 lb.) can spinach, well
  drained, or equivalent
  fresh spinach

4 eggs
¼ teaspoon salt
¼ teaspoon pepper
¼ teaspoon nutmeg
1 tablespoon grated
  Parmesan cheese

Heat oven to 350°. Mix onion and milk and let stand 3 minutes. Spoon corned beef hash into greased 9-inch pie plate; spread over bottom and sides to form a pie shell. Spoon spinach over hash. Beat together eggs, milk mixture, salt, pepper, and nutmeg. Pour over spinach and mix together lightly. Bake 40 to 45 minutes, or until custard is set. Sprinkle with Parmesan cheese before serving. Makes 6 servings.

❀ *Tongue and Macaroni*

1½ cups elbow macaroni
1 can condensed cream of celery soup
½ cup milk
1 cup cooked or canned peas
1 teaspoon prepared mustard

¼ cup pickle relish
2 (6 oz.) cans tongue, thinly sliced
½ cup coarsely shredded Swiss cheese

Cook macaroni according to package directions; drain. Preheat oven to 350°. Fold together macaroni, soup, milk, peas, mustard, pickle relish, and tongue. Pour into 1½-quart casserole; sprinkle with grated cheese. Cover and bake 15 minutes; uncover and bake 20 to 25 minutes, or until well heated. Makes 6 servings.

CHICKEN

Somebody once said chickens are like utility stocks—a foolproof investment.

With its high protein and low fat content, chicken gives you superb nourishment for your dollar. It is a good buy at any time of the year because the cost per pound of cooked edible meat is less than beef, pork, or turkey (which happens to have a bigger carcass, hence more waste).

We doubt that it would come as a surprise to anyone that chicken is a marvelously versatile budget stretcher—not judging by the number of times we've encountered chicken when dining out at friends' homes. Going to have a mob over? Chicken Barbecue. Entertaining the boss and his wife? Breasts of Chicken Supreme. A birthday party for teen-aged Susan? Chickenburgers. Afternoon bridge with the girls? What else but pineapple-banana-chicken salad. There's no end to the challenges you can meet with a chicken on hand.

The question is, does the homemaker always make the proper choice when she shops for chicken? She does if she knows a chicken's pedigree. The highest quality is U. S. Grade A, which means the chicken is fully fleshed, meaty, well finished, and attractive in appearance—a smooth, light-yellow skin is the key. Tender young chickens will be labeled as young chicken, Rock Cornish game hen, broiler, fryer, roaster, or capon. They're for you if you're planning to barbecue, fry, broil, or roast your purchase. Older, less tender chickens may be labeled mature chicken, old chicken, hen, stewing chicken, or fowl.

Never buy a chicken under two pounds. It won't be fully fleshed and plump with meaty drumsticks. And always take a close look at its color. If it is too white, it has probably been improperly processed and has lost its natural skin oils. If it is too yellow, it has too much fat. The ideal color is creamy, like rich eggnog.

Whole chicken is five or six cents per pound cheaper than cut-up chicken; fancy grades in parts may cost you 25 percent more. Chicken and turkey have become good buys in recent years; take the opportunity whenever they are offered as specials. Don't forget that you are buying servings. With a boneless roast at 90 cents a pound and chicken at 40 cents, you can figure that they will both end up costing about 30 cents a serving.

If you have a freezer, your very best buy is to take home three or four whole broiler-fryers. Cut them up yourself, wrap, and freeze them, and you'll be secure in the knowledge that you have four meals at the ready.

Cutting up whole chickens yourself is sound business; you save pennies per pound. Use the meat part for oven frying and the backs, wing tips, and necks for soup stock. Always freeze like parts together. In that way, you can have drumsticks, breasts, or wings whenever you want. Here's how to cut up a bird: Using chicken shears, cut off the leg and separate at joint into drumstick and second joint. Cut off the wing, remove the tip, separate wing at middle joint. Separate wishbone with meat on it from breast. Cut through ribs on either side and separate breast from the back. Cut the breast in half lengthwise and the back through the middle, crosswise. The side bones may be cut apart lengthwise with a cleaver.

Contrary to popular opinion, chicken breasts are not a luxury item because they contain practically no waste; you get what you pay for. You can, of course, master the technique of boning chicken breasts in your own kitchen and save the butcher's fee. Pick up your chicken shears again and try this method of boning to obtain the type of chicken breast usually identified in recipes as "supreme." Place chicken breast on a flat surface, skin side up. Cut in half or leave whole. Using fingers, pull off skin. If breast is whole, turn it over and flatten by pressing down on it. With paring knife, make small cut between meat and breastbone, at thinnest part of outer edge of breast. Using fingers and knife, pull and scrape meat away from bones. If the tendon, which runs about two thirds of the way down the center of the breast, has not been removed by the butcher, slip knife under it gently and remove. Trim ragged edges and flatten breast. Freeze if not using immediately.

Chicken is very perishable and should be treated with care. Always keep it under refrigeration until used. Remove the celophane wrapping before storing, cover loosely, and place in the coldest part of the refrigerator. If storing chicken for more than a day, freeze. Cook unfrozen chicken within two days.

Roasting chickens should be stuffed just before roasting. Never allow cooked chicken gravy or stuffing to stand at room temperature; refrigerate at once. To store, take the stuffing out of the bird. Wrap cooked chicken loosely in wax paper or foil. Plan to use it up within two or three days.

As long as it is kept solidly frozen and closely wrapped, frozen chicken keeps for four to eight months. But always cook it as soon as it is thawed. Leftover cooked chicken is easier to freeze and use if cut from the bones. Use it within three months.

Some weekend you may be out for a drive and see a farm sign announcing "Fresh Killed Chickens." If you are able to persuade the front-seat driver to stop long enough to buy one, don't rush home and prepare it. Freshly killed poultry is tough if cooked shortly after it is killed; it should be refrigerated at least 24 hours before it is used.

Back in 1932 a political slogan promised a chicken in every pot. Today it takes no such endorsement to convince the homemaker that she should have several chickens in her freezer. Her budget dictates it. She knows that with chicken nothing is wasted. After the main dish, leftovers can go into chicken salad or chicken potpie, and even the carcass can go into the pot for soup.

If you are uncertain about how much chicken to buy, keep this in mind: for broiling, choose a 1½- to 2½-pound meaty bird with little fat; for frying or sautéeing, pick one up to 3½ pounds; for roasting, larger birds of 3 to 4 pounds do nicely. The older bird will be best used for fricasseeing, stewing, or simmering in that redolent soup pot.

By the way, it is a fact that the thoughtful Japanese hostess will serve her guests only the left drumstick, because it is the more tender. It seems that chickens stand around a lot in the barnyard—and always on their right leg, which toughens it.

❀ *Arroz con Pollo*

½ cup salad or olive oil
1 (3 lb.) chicken, cut into
  serving pieces
3 small onions, finely
  chopped
1 large green pepper,
  coarsely chopped
2 (16 oz.) cans tomatoes

2 tablespoons salt
½ teaspoon black pepper
½ teaspoon garlic powder
2 teaspoons paprika
5 cups boiling water
½ teaspoon powdered
  saffron (optional)
2 cups uncooked rice

Heat oil in a large, heavy skillet over moderate heat. Add chicken
pieces and brown well on all sides. Add onions and green pepper;
cook 5 minutes, stirring frequently. Add tomatoes, salt, pepper,
garlic powder, and paprika; cook 15 minutes. Add boiling water,
rice, and saffron. Cover and cook over low heat for 45 minutes, stirring occasionally to prevent rice from sticking to skillet. Makes 4
to 6 servings.

❀ *Baked Chicken Legs and Mushrooms*

¼ cup margarine
8 chicken legs with thighs
  (3 lbs.)
¼ cup flour
1 (1 lb.) can whole onions,
  drained
1 (4 oz.) can chopped
  mushrooms, drained
1 small can evaporated
  milk, undiluted (⅔ cup)

1 (10½ oz.) can condensed
  cream of mushroom soup,
  undiluted
4 oz. sharp Cheddar cheese,
  grated (1 cup)
⅛ teaspoon pepper
paprika

Preheat oven to 425°. Melt margarine in a 13 by 9 by 2 inch baking
dish. Wash chicken legs and drain on paper towels. Coat completely with flour. Place, skin side down, in margarine in pan. Bake,
uncovered, 30 minutes. Turn pieces; bake 15 to 20 minutes longer,
or until chicken is well browned. Remove from oven. Reduce oven
temperature to 325°. Add onions and mushrooms. In medium bowl,
combine evaporated milk, soup, cheese, and pepper; mix until well
blended. Pour over chicken and vegetables; sprinkle with paprika.

Cover pan with foil. Bake 15 to 20 minutes, or until sauce is bubbly and hot. Makes 4 servings.

❀ *Breast of Chicken Madras*

3 chicken breasts, split
salt
pepper
¼ cup salad oil
2 pounds cooked or canned
  yams

1 (8 oz.) can tomato sauce
  with mushrooms
½ cup applesauce
½ teaspoon rosemary
¼ teaspoon cinnamon
1 clove garlic, minced

If desired, bone breasts; sprinkle with salt and pepper. Brown quickly in hot salad oil. Arrange skin side up with yams in 2½-quart baking dish. Combine tomato sauce, applesauce, rosemary, cinnamon, garlic. Spoon over chicken and yams. Bake at 375° for 30 to 35 minutes. Makes 6 servings.

❀ *Calico Chicken*

1 (3 lb.) broiler-fryer, cut
  up
¼ cup seasoned flour
¼ cup salad oil
1 (8 oz.) can tomato sauce
½ cup chicken broth

1 (12 oz.) can whole kernel
  corn with sweet peppers,
  drained
2 tablespoons parsley,
  chopped

Coat chicken pieces with seasoned flour. Brown in large skillet in salad oil. Drain fat. Add tomato sauce and chicken broth and simmer, covered, 40 minutes. Stir in corn and parsley. Simmer, covered, 10 minutes more. Makes 4 to 6 servings.

❀ Cheese-Fried Chicken

1 (2 to 2½ lb.) frying
  chicken, cut in pieces
½ cup corn flake crumbs
½ cup grated Parmesan
  cheese
¼ cup fresh chopped
  parsley
1 clove garlic, finely
  chopped

2 teaspoons salt
¼ teaspoon pepper
1 egg
1 tablespoon milk
shortening and butter or
  margarine, for frying

Heat oven to 325°. Wash and dry chicken thoroughly. Combine
corn flake crumbs, Parmesan cheese, parsley, garlic, salt, and pepper. Beat egg and milk together. Dip chicken pieces first in egg
mixture, then in crumb mixture to coat evenly. In heavy skillet over
moderate heat melt enough shortening and butter, about half and
half, to make about 1 inch fat. When fat is hot, add coated chicken
pieces, a few at a time, and brown evenly on all sides. As they are
browned, remove pieces to shallow baking pan. When all the pieces
have been browned, place pan in oven and bake about 30 minutes,
or until chicken is tender. Makes 4 servings.

❀ Chicken Cacciatore

3 pounds chicken parts
¼ cup salad oil
1 cup finely chopped onion
¾ cup chopped celery
1 clove garlic, minced

2 (8 oz.) cans tomato sauce
½ cup water
1 teaspoon salt
¼ teaspoon pepper
½ teaspoon basil

In skillet brown chicken in salad oil; remove and reserve. To skillet add onion, celery, and garlic; cook lightly. Return chicken to
skillet along with remaining ingredients. Simmer, uncovered, 30 to
40 minutes. Makes 4 to 6 servings. Good served with spaghetti.

🌸 Chicken Enchiladas

1 (6 oz.) can tomato paste
2 cups water
1 clove garlic, minced
1 tablespoon chili powder
½ teaspoon salt
½ teaspoon oregano
½ teaspoon ground cumin
  (optional)

10 corn tortillas
2 cups diced cooked
  chicken
½ cup chopped green onions
2 cups shredded Monterey
  Jack or mild Cheddar
  cheese

In saucepan combine tomato paste, water, garlic, chili powder, salt, oregano, and cumin; simmer 20 minutes. Dip tortillas quickly into hot sauce. Sprinkle chicken, onions, and cheese down center of each tortilla; spoon one tablespoon of sauce on each. Fold or roll tortilla around filling; place in greased 13 by 9 by 2 inch baking dish. Top with remaining sauce and cheese. Bake at 350° for 20 minutes. Makes 5 servings.

🌸 Chicken Goody

½ pound pork sausage links,
  cut into chunks
1 (3 lb.) frying chicken,
  cut up
1 (14½ oz.) can stewed
  tomatoes

¾ cup water
1 teaspoon salt
1 cup raw regular rice
¼ cup grated Parmesan
  cheese

Lightly brown sausage in large skillet; then brown chicken in same skillet. Remove fat. Add remaining ingredients except cheese. Cover and simmer 45 minutes; stir occasionally. Sprinkle with cheese. Makes 6 servings.

❁ Chicken Kiev

½ cup butter
1 clove garlic, minced
2 teaspoons chopped chives
2 teaspoons chopped
    parsley
½ teaspoon salt
3 large chicken breasts,
    split, skinned, and boned

1 egg
1 tablespoon water
¼ cup flour
¾ cup dry bread crumbs
salad oil

Combine butter, garlic, chives, parsley, and salt; on waxed paper form into ¾-inch roll. Wrap; chill until very hard. With rolling pin, gently flatten chicken breast to ¼-inch thickness, taking care not to tear chicken. Cut butter roll into 6 slices; place one slice on center of each piece of chicken. Roll up tightly, tucking in ends; tie with string. In shallow bowl blend egg and water; place flour on one square of waxed paper, crumbs on another. Dip chicken first in flour, shaking off excess, then in egg, and finally in crumbs, coating well. Chill thoroughly. In skillet heat salad oil, 1½ inches deep, to 370°. Fry chicken, turning occasionally, until golden brown. Makes 6 servings.

❁ Chicken Marengo

6 chicken legs with thighs
    (about 3 lbs.)
2 tablespoons salad oil
1 clove garlic, peeled
1 (8 oz.) can whole onions,
    drained
1 (1 lb. 12 oz.) can
    tomatoes, with liquid
1 (6 oz.) can sliced mush-
    rooms, with liquid

2 chicken bouillon cubes
4 sprigs parsley
1 bay leaf
1 teaspoon salt
¼ teaspoon pepper
¼ teaspoon dried thyme
    leaves
⅓ cup dry white wine
3 tablespoons flour

Wash chicken; dry with paper towels. Brown garlic in hot oil in Dutch oven. Remove garlic and discard. Add chicken to hot oil and sauté until golden brown on all sides. Add onions, tomatoes, mushrooms, bouillon cubes, parsley, bay leaf, salt, pepper, and thyme. Bring to boil. Reduce heat and simmer, covered, one hour, or until chicken is tender. In small bowl, stir wine into flour to make a smooth paste; stir into chicken mixture; bring to boil, stirring constantly. Reduce heat and simmer five minutes longer. Makes 3 to 6 servings.

❀ Chicken Tamale Pie

½ cup chopped onion
½ cup sliced celery
1 clove garlic, crushed
3 tablespoons salad oil
1½ cups slivered or diced
   cooked chicken
1 (8 oz.) can tomato sauce

1 (2¼ oz.) can chopped ripe
   olives
2½ cups chicken broth
2 teaspoons salt
2 teaspoons chili powder
1 cup corn meal
1 cup cold water

In skillet lightly cook onion, celery, and garlic in 2 tablespoons salad oil. Stir in chicken, tomato sauce, olives, ½ cup chicken broth, 1 teaspoon salt, and chili powder. In saucepan bring remaining chicken broth to boil; add remaining salt and salad oil. Mix corn meal and cold water; gradually stir into boiling broth. Cook over low heat, stirring constantly, until mixture is quite thick; pour half into oiled 2-quart casserole. Cover with chicken mixture; top with remaining corn meal. Bake at 350° for 45 minutes. Makes 4 servings.

❀ Chicken Wings in Orange Sauce

1¼ pounds chicken wings
2 tablespoons flour
⅛ teaspoon ground savory
¾ teaspoon salt
few grains pepper
2 tablespoons shortening

1 cup orange juice
½ teaspoon sugar
water
2 tablespoons slivered
   toasted almonds

Wash and dry chicken wings. Mix flour, savory, salt, and pepper. Coat chicken wings with mixture and save leftover flour mixture for gravy. Melt shortening in skillet and brown chicken wings lightly on all sides over moderate heat. Pour orange juice over chicken. Cover and simmer 15 to 20 minutes, until tender. Remove wings and keep warm. Combine leftover flour mixture with sugar. Stir in enough water to make a smooth paste. Gradually stir into liquid in skillet and cook over low heat until thickened. Stir in almonds. Serve with chicken wings. Makes 2 servings.

🌼 Chinese Chicken

1 (4 to 5 lb.) ready-to-cook roasting chicken
1 tablespoon soy sauce
1½ cups coarsely chopped celery
¼ cup chopped parsley
1 teaspoon salt
4 tablespoons butter or margarine

⅔ cup cooked rice
¼ cup shopped onion
6 medium mushrooms, coarsely chopped
⅓ cup honey
¼ cup softened unsalted butter

Heat oven to 450°. Wash and dry chicken thoroughly. Brush inside of chicken with soy sauce. In large mixing bowl combine celery, parsley, and salt. Melt 4 tablespoons butter in a skillet over low heat; add rice, onion, and mushrooms. Cook and stir until rice is golden but not brown. Add to celery mixture. Blend thoroughly. Stuff the chicken with this mixture. Truss and place chicken in shallow baking pan lined with aluminum foil. Combine honey and unsalted butter; beat with a rotary beater until light and foamy. Spread this mixture evenly over chicken. Place in oven. Bake at 450° about 30 minutes. During this time, turn bird from side to side and baste frequently with honey-butter mixture in bottom of pan. Skin will get very dark brown. Cover loosely with foil, reduce oven temperature to 350°, and continue to bake an additional 15–20 minutes per pound, until tender. Makes 6 servings.

🌼 Confetti Chicken

1 (2½ to 3 lb.) frying chicken, cut up
¼ cup flour
1½ teaspoons salt
¼ teaspoon pepper
¼ cup salad oil
½ cup chicken stock, bouillon, or water

2 tablespoons chopped parsley
1 (12 oz.) can corn, drained
1 tablespoon chopped green pepper
1 (8 oz.) can tomato sauce minced onion

Coat chicken with combination of flour, salt, and pepper. Brown chicken in salad oil in large skillet. Pour off excess fat. Add stock, cover, and simmer 40 minutes. Add parsley, corn, green pepper, tomato sauce, and onion. Simmer 10 minutes, or until chicken is tender. Makes 4 servings.

❀ Crunchy Oven-Fried Chicken

¼ cup milk
1 egg, beaten slightly
1 teaspoon salt
¼ teaspoon pepper
1 teaspoon paprika
1 cup finely crushed corn flakes

1 (2½ to 3 lb.) frying chicken, cut up
salt
flour
⅓ cup salad oil

Combine milk and egg in shallow dish. Blend salt, pepper, and paprika with corn flakes in another shallow dish. Salt chicken lightly, coat with flour, dip in milk-egg mixture, then roll in corn flake mixture. Arrange, skin side down, on bottom of shallow baking pan covered with salad oil. Bake at 375° 30 minutes. Turn chicken and bake 20 to 25 minutes longer, until brown and tender. Makes 4 to 6 servings.

❀ Drumsticks Italian Style

6 chicken drumsticks
6 chicken thighs
¼ cup salad oil
salt
pepper
1 onion, sliced

1 bay leaf
½ teaspoon oregano
1 (6 oz.) can tomato paste
1 cup water
1 cup macaroni, cooked and drained

In skillet brown chicken pieces in salad oil; pour off fat. Sprinkle with salt and pepper; add onion, bay leaf, and oregano. Mix tomato paste, water, and ½ teaspoon salt. Pour over chicken; simmer, covered, 30 minutes; remove bay leaf. Stir in macaroni and cook 10 minutes more. Makes 6 servings.

❀ *Fricassee with Dumplings*

6 to 8 chicken wings
3 tablespoons salad oil
salt
pepper
1 cup sliced carrots
½ cup sliced celery

¼ cup chopped onion
1 cup chicken broth
½ cup milk
2 tablespoons flour
Dumplings

In skillet brown chicken in salad oil; pour off fat. Sprinkle with salt and pepper; add carrots, celery, onion, chicken broth, and ½ teaspoon salt. Simmer covered, 15 minutes. Meanwhile, blend milk and flour. Stir into chicken and simmer until thickened. Prepare dumplings and drop over chicken. Simmer, uncovered, 10 minutes; cover skillet and cook 10 minutes more. Makes 2 to 3 servings.

DUMPLINGS: Sift 1 cup sifted all-purpose flour, 2 teaspoons baking powder, and ½ teaspoon salt into mixing bowl. Pour ½ cup milk and 3 tablespoons salad oil into measuring cup; pour all at once into flour. Stir lightly until well mixed. Drop by tablespoonfuls over simmering chicken mixture.

❀ *Fricasseed Chicken Wings*

12 chicken wings
1 medium onion
4 whole cloves
1 bay leaf
1 teaspoon salt
4 sprigs parsley
3 tablespoons butter or
  margarine

4 tablespoons flour
½ cup evaporated milk
1 teaspoon lemon juice
½ teaspoon salt
⅛ teaspoon nutmeg
2 tablespoons chopped
  parsley

Place chicken wings in heavy saucepan. Add next 5 ingredients and just enough water to cover wings. Cook over medium heat until chicken is fork tender, about 45 minutes. Remove wings and keep warm. Melt butter in a saucepan over low heat; stir in flour. Gradually add 1½ cups of the strained chicken broth, stirring constantly till thickened. Blend in milk, lemon juice, salt, and nutmeg; pour over chicken. Top with parsley. Makes 4 servings.

❁ *Front Porch Chicken Supper*

8 chicken drumsticks
salt
pepper
2 tablespoons salad oil
1 cup chopped onion
½ cup snipped parsley
1 (1 lb. 13 oz.) can whole
  potatoes, drained

2 (8 oz.) cans tomato sauce
  with mushrooms
⅓ cup water
¼ teaspoon salt
½ teaspoon thyme
¼ teaspoon sugar

Sprinkle drumsticks with salt and pepper; brown in salad oil in skillet. Add onion, parsley, and potatoes and brown lightly. Add tomato sauce, water, salt, thyme, and sugar. Cover and simmer until chicken is done, about 30 minutes. Makes 4 servings.

❁ *Green Pepper-Chicken Paprika*

GREEN PEPPERS:

6 medium green peppers
  (2 lbs.)
3 quarts water

1 tablespoon salt
¾ cup raw long-grain white
  rice

CHICKEN PAPRIKA:

3 tablespoons margarine
1 cup thinly sliced onion
½ teaspoon salt
2 teaspoons paprika
1 (10½ oz.) can cream of
  chicken soup, undiluted

3 cups cut-up cooked
  chicken (about 1 lb.)
½ cup commercial sour
  cream

GREEN PEPPERS: Wash peppers. Cut ½-inch-thick slice from tops; cut out stem. Chop slices; set aside. Scoop out seeds and ribs from peppers. In large kettle, bring water and salt to boil. Add whole peppers; reduce heat and simmer, uncovered, 10 to 15 minutes, or until peppers are tender. Drain. Meanwhile, cook rice as package label directs. Drain. Preheat oven to 350°.

CHICKEN PAPRIKA: In hot margarine in skillet, sauté onion, reserved chopped green pepper, salt, and paprika until onion is golden—5 to 8 minutes. Remove from heat. Stir in chicken soup; bring to boil, stirring constantly. Stir in chicken; remove from heat. Stir in sour cream.

Place peppers in shallow baking dish. Spoon rice into peppers, dividing evenly. Fill with chicken paprika. Cover dish with foil. Bake 35 minutes, or until filled peppers are heated through. Sprinkle with paprika if desired. Makes 6 servings.

❁ *Ginger Broiled Chicken*

1 (1½ to 2 lb.) broiling   2 teaspoons ground ginger
    chicken, split in half   ½ cup salad oil
juice of 1 lemon   2 teaspoons salt

Wash and dry chicken. Place in shallow pan. Combine remaining ingredients; pour over chicken. Cover and marinate 4 hours. Place chicken skin side down on broiler rack. Broil 5 to 7 inches from heat. When chicken starts to brown, turn and brush with marinade. Continue to broil, turning and basting often, until fork tender, about 40 minutes. Makes 2 servings.

❁ *Harvest Chicken*

1 (2½ to 3 lb.) frying   1 tart apple, pared, cored,
    chicken, cut up   and cut in thin wedges
½ cup flour   1 bay leaf
salad oil to depth of 1 inch   1 (8 oz.) can tomato sauce
    in skillet   1 cup water
1 small green pepper, thinly   1½ teaspoons salt
    sliced   ¼ teaspoon pepper

Coat chicken with flour and brown in salad oil. Remove. Drain off all but 2 tablespoons drippings and browned bits. Combine remaining ingredients in skillet with chicken. Cover; simmer 40 minutes. Makes 4 servings.

❦ *Italian-Style Chicken*

1 (2½ to 3 lb.) frying
  chicken, cut up
¼ cup flour
1 teaspoon salt
¼ teaspoon pepper
2 tablespoons salad oil

1 clove garlic, crushed
¼ teaspoon oregano
2 (8 oz.) cans tomato sauce
½ cup chicken bouillon
1 onion, sliced

Lightly coat chicken with mixture of flour, salt, and pepper. Brown in large skillet in salad oil. Combine garlic and remaining ingredients and pour over chicken. Cover and simmer about 45 minutes, until chicken is tender. Makes 4 servings.

❦ *Maryland Company Chicken*

1 (2½ to 3 lb.) broiler-
  fryer, cut up
3 tablespoons flour
1 teaspoon salt
⅛ teaspoon pepper

½ cup salad oil
½ teaspoon dried rosemary
3 tablespoons dry white
  wine or lemon juice

Put flour, salt, and pepper in paper bag; drop in chicken, 2 or 3 pieces at a time, and shake until well coated. In skillet brown in salad oil at medium heat. Sprinkle with rosemary; add wine. Simmer, covered, about 40 minutes. Makes 4 servings.

❦ *Oven-Barbecued Chicken*

¼ cup salad oil
¼ cup ketchup
¼ cup lemon juice
2 tablespoons Worcester-
  shire sauce

1 (2½ to 3 lb.) frying
  chicken, cut up
salt
pepper

In saucepan, combine salad oil, ketchup, lemon juice, and Worcestershire. Bring to boil and remove from heat. Season chicken with salt and pepper and arrange in a baking pan; pour on sauce. Bake at 350° for 45 minutes to 1 hour, turning chicken frequently. Makes 4 servings.

❊ *Pineapple Braised Chicken*

1 (2½ to 3 lb.) broiler-
  fryer, cut up
⅓ cup unsifted all-purpose
  flour
½ teaspoon salt
⅛ teaspoon pepper
¼ cup salad oil
1 clove garlic, crushed
¼ cup sliced onion
⅓ cup coarsely chopped
  green pepper

½ teaspoon dry mustard
1 tablespoon soy sauce
1 (12 oz.) can unsweetened
  pineapple juice
⅓ cup chili sauce
1 (13½ oz.) can pineapple
  chunks, drained
1 (11 oz.) can mandarin
  orange sections, drained

Rinse chicken in cold water; dry on paper towels. Combine flour, salt, and pepper. Roll chicken pieces in flour mixture, coating well. In hot oil in large skillet sauté chicken pieces, turning, until golden brown. Remove chicken as it browns to 3-quart casserole. Preheat oven to 350°. Drain fat from skillet, leaving 1 tablespoonful. Add garlic, onion, green pepper; sauté until tender. Add mustard, soy sauce, pineapple juice, and chili sauce; bring to boil, stirring to dissolve browned bits in pan. Reduce heat; simmer, uncovered, about 5 minutes, or until slightly thickened. Pour sauce over chicken in casserole; bake, covered, 30 minutes. Add drained pineapple chunks and orange sections, and baste with liquid in casserole. Bake, uncovered, 15 minutes, or until chicken is tender. Serve with hot rice. Makes 4 servings.

❊ *Pot-Roasted Chicken*

1 (4 lb.) chicken, cut up
1 cup minced onion
¼ cup salad oil
1 teaspoon salt
¼ teaspoon pepper
1 teaspoon paprika

½ teaspoon rosemary
¼ teaspoon garlic powder
1 teaspoon flour
1 (8 oz.) can tomato sauce
  with mushrooms
1 cup boiling water

Brown chicken and onion in salad oil. Add remaining ingredients. Cover and simmer for 1 hour, or until chicken is tender. Makes 6 servings.

❀ Skillet Chicken Barbecue

1 (2½ to 3 lb.) broiler-
fryer, cut up
¼ cup flour
1 teaspoon salt
¼ teaspoon pepper
3 tablespoons salad oil
1 (8 oz.) can tomato sauce
with onions

½ cup water
2 tablespoons vinegar
1 tablespoon brown sugar
1 teaspoon Worcestershire
sauce
½ teaspoon salt

Coat chicken with flour, 1 teaspoon salt, and pepper. In skillet brown in salad oil over medium heat; pour off fat. Combine remaining ingredients, pour over chicken. Cover; simmer, basting several times, 45 minutes, or until chicken is tender. Makes 4 servings.

❀ Spicy Chicken 'n Fruit

3 whole chicken breasts,
split
salad oil
1 teaspoon salt
⅛ teaspoon pepper
1 (15 oz.) can peach or
apricot halves

1 (8 oz.) can tomato sauce
with mushrooms
½ teaspoon cinnamon or
nutmeg
1 teaspoon whole cloves

Brush chicken with salad oil; sprinkle with salt and pepper. Arrange, skin side down, in 13 by 9 by 2 inch baking pan. Bake at 375° for 20 minutes. Meanwhile, drain syrup from fruit into saucepan; stir in tomato sauce and cinnamon; simmer 5 minutes. Turn chicken; pour on half of sauce. Bake at 325° for 20 minutes more. Turn chicken; pour on remaining sauce. Stud fruit with cloves and arrange around chicken. Bake 10 to 15 minutes more, basting occasionally, until fruit is thoroughly heated. Makes 6 servings.

❁ *Texas-Style Barbecued Chicken*

2 (1½ to 2 lb.) broiler-
fryers, split or quartered
salad oil
1 (8 oz.) can tomato sauce
1 medium onion, thinly
sliced
1 tablespoon Worcester-
shire sauce

2 teaspoons prepared
mustard
2 teaspoons sugar
½ teaspoon chili powder
1 clove garlic, crushed

Place chicken on broiler rack; brush with salad oil. Broil chicken 8 to 10 inches from heat for 50 to 60 minutes, turning occasionally, until done. Meanwhile, combine remaining ingredients. Baste chicken with sauce during last 10 minutes of cooking time. Makes 4 servings.

FISH

People who are watching their waistlines develop a great fondness for fish: with fish one counts bones, not calories. But people who have their eyes on their pocketbooks should also include fish in their circle of intimate foods.

Bursting with proteins and very tasty if not overcooked, fish can be a good buy even when *not* on sale. That is because it has so little waste.

Naturally, fish is freshest and cheapest at the waterfront where it comes in, but you may not always be able to hie yourself to a fisherman's wharf. You'll just have to play Izaak Walton at your local fish market. It can be a rewarding experience if you know what you're looking for.

If you have the courage, always look a fish in the eye: that is the best way to judge its freshness. Fresh fish will have eyes that are bright and bulging, not glassy and sunken. The flesh should be firm and elastic, with scales clinging to the flesh; the gills should be reddish and with no unpleasant odor. (We confine *our* stares to the display of frozen fish fillets and avoid those fellows that look as if they should be mounted on plaques in The Jolly Anchor Inn.)

How much fish you buy—fresh or frozen—depends on the form you choose. Whole fish is just as it comes from the water; you will need one pound per serving. Drawn fish is whole but eviscerated; again, allow one pound per serving. Dressed fish is eviscerated and scaled, with head, tail, and fins removed; allow ½ pound per serving. Steaks are cross-section slices, cut about ¾ inch thick; allow ½ pound per serving. Fillets, the sides of the fish, are cut lengthwise away from the backbone. Plan on ⅓ to ½ pound per serving.

Since dressed fish is 45 percent edible, steaks 85 percent edible, and fillets 100 percent edible, you can readily see why fillets are your most economical buy, although the price per pound may be higher.

There are also fish "sticks" on the market—uniform cuts from frozen blocks of fish fillets. They are coated with batter, breaded, partially cooked, packaged, and frozen. Allow ⅓ to ½ pound per serving. But do keep in mind that frozen fish is not as thrifty a choice when it's breaded—you are liable to get more breading than fish.

Everybody knows that lobster, crab, and shrimp are the Cadillacs, minks, and emeralds of the seafood world. But even these luxury treats have their moments for the thrifty homemaker. A big catch, for example, may make prices tumble. A manager may want to get rid of his seafood supply quickly and not keep it over a weekend. Whatever the reason, it is worthwhile to keep an eye on this special trio and take advantage of any price breaks. Don't ever buy fresh shrimp that are precooked; you can get better results at home by cooking your own shrimp in a little salted, boiling water with a celery stalk and bay leaf thrown in. And you will save better than half the price!

Speaking of shrimp, compare prices from market to market on those plastic bags of frozen shrimp. Every once in a while you will discover a real bargain. This gives you a chance to have a shrimp cocktail now and then and keep the unused shrimp in the freezer.

Canned fish? It's the careful cook's stand-by, especially salmon and tuna. Tuna is often used as a weekend special to lure shoppers to a market. That is the time to stock up. Tuna lends itself beautifully to a vast number of thrifty dishes, particularly casseroles and salads.

If you buy frozen fish, the best way to defrost it is to place it in the refrigerator and let it remain there until pliable enough to handle. At 40° it will take about 18 hours for a 1-pound fillet to thaw. The fastest way to defrost fish is to cover it with cold, *running* water; the length of time required will depend on the size and shape of the fish. Steaks or fillets will thaw out in about 30 minutes in cold running water. It is never wise to leave frozen fish at room temperature to thaw. The thinner parts of the fish will thaw more quickly than the thicker and spoilage can set in.

Most fish, being comparatively bland in flavor, take their character from their preparation and the sauces mated with them. Whether you steam, poach, fry, boil, broil, or bake fish, don't overdo it. Fish does not need cooking to tenderize it; it is done when it flakes easily with a fork. Start using your fork to test it at half the given cooking time.

If you like a recipe but can't find the fish, don't hesitate to cook the fish available. Ninety-eight percent of all fish recipes are interchangeable. And don't try to keep a Social Register for fish. They have regional names, which makes it all very baffling. Fluke here is summer flounder there; sea trout is weakfish; striped bass is rockfish. Enough of that. It's consoling to think that once a can of tuna, always a can of tuna.

✿ *Baked Fillets Thermidor*

2 pounds sole fillets
5 tablespoons butter or
* margarine*
2 teaspoons salt
¼ teaspoon pepper
½ teaspoon seasoned salt

1¼ cups milk
3 tablespoons flour
1 cup grated sharp Cheddar
* cheese (¼ lb.)*
3 tablespoons dry sherry
paprika

Preheat oven to 350°. Wash fillets and dry on paper towels. Melt 2 tablespoons butter. Use to brush dark side of fillets. Sprinkle with salt, pepper, and seasoned salt. Roll up fillets, seasonings inside. Arrange in a 9 by 9 by 1¾ inch baking dish. Pour on ½ cup milk; bake, uncovered, 30 minutes. Meanwhile, in medium saucepan melt rest of butter. Remove from heat. Add flour, stirring until smooth. Gradually stir in remaining ¾ cup milk; bring to boil, stirring constantly. Reduce heat. Add cheese, stirring until it is melted; then add sherry. Carefully drain liquid from fish; stir liquid into cheese sauce. Pour sauce over fish. Sprinkle with paprika. Place under broiler, 4 inches from heat, until sauce is golden brown. Makes 6 servings.

✿ *Baked Fish in Herb Sauce*

1 pound fish fillets
salt
pepper
1 (8 oz.) can tomato sauce
¼ cup water

2 tablespoons salad oil
1 teaspoon lemon juice
½ teaspoon basil
½ teaspoon thyme

Sprinkle fillets with salt and pepper. Place in shallow baking pan. In saucepan combine remaining ingredients; bring to boil and simmer

5 minutes. Pour over fish. Bake at 375° for 30 minutes, basting occasionally. Makes 3 to 4 servings.

❀ *Baked Sole Provençale*

2 (*12 oz.*) *packages frozen sole fillets*	1 *teaspoon salt*
5 *tablespoons butter or margarine*	⅛ *teaspoon pepper*
1 *cup chopped onion*	1 (*1 lb.*) *can tomatoes, undrained*
½ *cup thinly sliced celery*	1½ *cups soft white bread cubes*
2 *tablespoons flour*	¼ *teaspoon oregano*

Let fish thaw in package ½ hour or as package label directs. Meanwhile, in 3 tablespoons hot butter in medium skillet sauté onion and celery until tender—about 5 minutes. Remove from heat; stir in flour, ½ teaspoon salt, and the pepper until well blended. Gradually stir in tomatoes. Bring to boil, stirring constantly. Reduce heat and simmer 1 minute. Preheat oven to 375°. Cut each package of fish into thirds to make 3 serving-size pieces. Place in single layer in shallow 1½-quart baking dish (12 by 8 by 2 inches). Sprinkle with ½ teaspoon salt. Spoon tomato mixture over all. Bake, covered, 30 minutes. Melt remaining butter, stir in bread cubes and oregano. Sprinkle over fish. Bake, uncovered, 20 minutes longer, or until fish flakes easily with fork. Makes 5 to 6 servings.

❀ *Baked Stuffed Whole Fish*

1 (*3 to 5 lb.*) *whole fish, dressed and split* (*haddock, cod, bluefish, or similar fish*)	*salt*
	pepper
	2 *tablespoons butter or margarine, melted*

STUFFING:

1 *egg, beaten*	½ *cup butter or margarine, melted*
¼ *teaspoon dried thyme leaves*	3 *tablespoons finely chopped onion*
½ *teaspoon dill seed*	2 *tablespoons hot water*
2 *tablespoons chopped parsley*	3 *cups white bread crumbs* (*day-old bread, grated*)
¼ *teaspoon salt*	
dash pepper	

Preheat oven to 500°.

STUFFING: Combine egg, thyme, dill seed, parsley, salt, and pepper
in large bowl; mix well. In hot butter sauté onion until golden. To
seasonings add onion-butter mixture, hot water, and bread crumbs,
tossing lightly with fork; mix well.

Sprinkle inside of fish with salt and pepper. Place fish in large shallow baking dish; stuff; close opening with skewers or toothpicks.
Brush top with 2 tablespoons melted butter. Bake, uncovered, for
10 minutes. Reduce heat to 400°; bake 10 minutes per pound, or
until fish flakes easily with fork. Makes 3 to 5 servings.

✿ *Barbecued Red Snapper Steaks*

2 *pounds red snapper steaks*   1 *tablespoon sugar*
   or fillets, fresh or frozen   1 *teaspoon salt*
1 *(6 oz.) can tomato paste*   ⅛ *teaspoon garlic salt*
⅓ *cup water*   1 *tablespoon salad oil*
2 *tablespoons lime juice*
2 *tablespoons Worcester-*
   shire sauce

Thaw fish, if frozen. Cut into serving-size portions. Combine remaining ingredients. Place fish on charcoal grill, about 4 inches from
medium hot coals, for 6 to 10 minutes. Brush several times with
sauce; turn and cook for 7 to 10 minutes longer, or until fish flakes
easily when tested with a fork. Makes 6 servings.

✿ *Batter-Fried Sea Squab*

2 *pounds sea squab*   ⅛ *teaspoon Tabasco*
   (blowfish)   ½ *cup all-purpose flour*
garlic salt   ¼ *teaspoon salt*
1 *egg*   ⅛ *teaspon dry mustard*
⅓ *cup milk*   *salad oil*

Rinse fish and pat dry with paper towels. Sprinkle lightly with garlic
salt and set aside. In a bowl beat egg slightly, then stir in milk and
Tabasco. Mix together flour, salt, and mustard. Stir into egg mixture
and beat until smooth. In heavy deep saucepan or electric skillet
heat oil to 375°. For best results have oil at least 1½ inches deep.
Coat fish with the batter and fry 3 to 5 minutes on each side, or
until well browned and fish flakes easily when tested with a fork.

This same batter may be used with other small fish fillets, shrimp, or scallops. Makes 4 to 6 servings.

❁ *Boiled Halibut*

1½ *pounds halibut or*
  whiting
1½ *teaspoons salt*
2 *cups water*
3 *peppercorns*

½ *clove garlic*
1 *sprig parsley*
½ *medium onion, sliced*
1 *bay leaf*

Cut fish into serving-size pieces and sprinkle well with salt. Place in a saucepan; add water and remaining ingredients. Bring to a boil over moderately low heat (about 225°); cover and simmer gently 15 to 20 minutes, or until fish is easily flaked with a fork. Do not boil. Makes 4 to 6 servings.

❁ *Clam Cakes*

2 (7½ *oz.*) *cans minced*
  clams
¼ *cup butter or margarine*
3 *cups packaged bread*
  stuffing
2 *tablespoons instant*
  minced onion

1 *tablespoon parsley flakes*
1 (8 *oz.*) *can tomato sauce*
1 *egg, beaten*
2 *tablespoons salad oil*
½ *cup mayonnaise*

Drain liquid from 1 can of clams into 2-quart saucepan; add butter and heat until butter melts. Stir in stuffing, onion, parsley, clams, and 2 tablespoons tomato sauce. Add egg and mix well. Shape into 8 cakes and chill for 30 minutes. Sauté cakes in salad oil until golden brown on both sides. Combine remaining tomato sauce with mayonnaise and heat over low heat. Serve over clam cakes. Makes 4 servings.

❀ Clam Fritters

2 (7½ or 8 oz.) cans minced
   clams
1 cup sifted all-purpose
   flour
1 teaspoon baking powder
¾ teaspoon salt

⅛ teaspoon nutmeg
dash pepper
1 egg, slightly beaten
⅓ cup milk
1 teaspoon onion juice
salad oil for deep-fat frying

Drain clams thoroughly and reserve 2 tablespoons of the liquid; set aside. Sift together into a bowl flour, baking powder, salt, nutmeg, and pepper. Combine egg, milk, onion juice, and the 2 tablespoons clam liquid; add to flour mixture and beat until smooth. Stir in drained clams. In heavy deep saucepan or electric skillet heat oil to 375°. Drop batter by level tablespoonfuls into hot oil. Fry 3 minutes or until well browned on all sides. Serve with chili or tartare sauce. Makes 20 to 25 fritters or 4 to 5 servings.

❀ Easy Baked Fish

1¼ pounds frozen or fresh
   haddock, halibut, bass, or
   cod fillets (about 4)
salt
pepper
¼ teaspoon basil or oregano

4 slices American cheese
1 (14½ oz.) can stewed
   tomatoes
⅔ cup fresh bread crumbs
1 tablespoon butter or
   margarine

Sprinkle fish with salt, pepper, and basil. Place a slice of cheese at end of each fillet; roll up and fasten with toothpick. Place in 1½-quart baking dish; pour stewed tomatoes over; sprinkle with crumbs and dot with butter. Bake at 375° for 30 minutes. Makes 4 servings.

✿ *Fish 'n Fries Roll-Ups*

1½ pounds fish fillets
2 tablespoons parsley flakes
1 teaspoon salt
⅛ teaspoon pepper
1 (9 oz.) package frozen
  French-fried potatoes

2 tablespoons melted butter
  or margarine
1 (8 oz.) can tomato sauce
1 clove garlic, crushed
½ teaspoon lemon juice
⅛ teaspoon poultry
  seasoning

Sprinkle fillets with parsley flakes, salt, and pepper. Place 5 to 6 French fries on each fillet; roll. Arrange in 10 by 6 by 1 inch baking dish; pour butter over fillets. Bake at 375° for 40 minutes. Meanwhile, in saucepan combine tomato sauce, garlic, lemon juice, and poultry seasoning; simmer 10 minutes. Pour over fillets and bake 5 minutes longer. Makes 5 to 6 servings.

✿ *Fish-Cheese Puff*

2 pounds haddock or
  halibut fillets
½ cup commercial sour
  cream
½ cup grated sharp Cheddar
  cheese

2 eggs, separated
2 tablespoons chopped
  pimiento-stuffed olives
1 tablespoon finely chopped
  onion
½ teaspoon salt

Preheat oven to 350°. Wash fillets and dry well on paper towels. Lightly grease a large shallow baking dish. Arrange fillets in single layer in dish. In medium bowl combine sour cream, cheese, egg yolks, olives, onion, and salt. In medium bowl beat egg whites with rotary beater until stiff peaks form. With rubber scraper, gently fold into sour cream mixture until well combined. Spread over fish, covering completely; bake, uncovered, 25 minutes. Puff will be golden. Serve from baking dish. Makes 6 servings.

🏵 Island Fish Skillet

1 (1 lb.) package frozen
   fish fillets, thawed
⅓ cup flour
½ teaspoon salt
⅛ teaspoon pepper
¼ cup salad oil
¾ cup sliced celery
½ cup chopped onion

1 clove garlic, crushed
2 cups cooked rice
1 (8¾ oz.) can pineapple
   tidbits, with liquid
2 tablespoons vinegar
2 tablespoons soy sauce
¼ cup snipped fresh
   parsley

Cut fillets into serving-sized pieces. Coat with mixture of flour, salt, and pepper. In skillet lightly brown fillets with celery, onion, and garlic in salad oil over medium heat. Remove fish from skillet. Stir in remaining ingredients except parsley. Return fish to skillet; simmer, covered, until thoroughly heated. Sprinkle with parsley. Makes 3 servings.

🏵 Italian Fish Fillets

2 pounds fish fillets
   (halibut, sole, or
   haddock)
¾ cup cracker crumbs
2 tablespoons salad oil
1 (8 oz.) can tomato sauce
   with cheese
2 tablespoons water
2 tablespoons chopped
   parsley

1 tablespoon minced onion
1 tablespoon chopped ripe
   olives
½ teaspoon garlic salt
¼ teaspoon oregano
¼ teaspoon pepper
pinch sugar
fresh parsley
lemon slices

Cut fillets in 5 to 6 serving pieces. Coat with crumbs; set aside. Meanwhile, combine all remaining ingredients except salad oil; simmer 10 minutes. Brown fish on both sides in hot oil; cook just until fish flakes. Place on hot serving platter and garnish with parsley and lemon slices. Spoon some of the tomato sauce over fish; pass rest. Makes 5 to 6 servings.

❋ Poached Codfish in Mustard Sauce

2½ pounds codfish steaks
2½ cups water
1 medium onion, quartered
1 bay leaf, crumbled
dash allspice
1¼ teaspoon salt
¼ teaspoon pepper

3 tablespoons butter or
  margarine
3 tablespoons flour
¼ cup prepared English-
  style mustard
1 tablespoon lemon juice

Wipe codfish with damp cloth. Arrange in single layer in large skillet with tight-fitting cover. Add water, onion, bay leaf, allspice, ¾ teaspoon salt, and the pepper; bring to boil. Reduce heat; simmer, covered, 8 minutes, or until fish flakes easily with fork. Carefully drain fish, reserving liquid. Place fish on heated platter; keep warm. Melt butter in medium saucepan. Remove from heat. Add flour, stirring until smooth. Gradually stir in 2 cups liquid reserved from fish; bring to boil, stirring. Reduce heat; stir in mustard, lemon juice, and remaining salt; simmer gently until heated through. Spoon some of sauce over codfish; pass rest. Makes 6 servings.

❋ Poached Fillet of Sole

1½ cups water
½ medium onion, sliced
1 bay leaf
1 tablespoon lemon juice
1 tablespoon vinegar

3 peppercorns
1 teaspoon salt
1 pound sole fillets
chopped fresh parsley

Place water, onion, bay leaf, lemon juice, vinegar, peppercorns, and salt in a saucepan; cook 5 minutes over moderate heat. Cut fish into serving-size pieces and add to the water. Cook over low heat 5 to 10 minutes, or until fish is easily flaked with a fork. Sprinkle fish with chopped parsley before serving. Makes 3 servings.

❀ Salmon Loaf

1 (1 lb.) can salmon, flaked
2 cups fresh bread crumbs
1 egg, beaten
½ cup milk
2 tablespoons chopped
  parsley

½ cup finely chopped celery
¼ teaspoon salt
¼ teaspoon Tabasco
2 tablespoons melted butter
  or margarine
2 tablespoons lemon juice

Preheat oven to 375°. Combine all ingredients and toss lightly with a fork. Turn into greased 9 by 5 by 3 inch loaf pan; smooth top. Bake in oven 45 to 50 minutes, or until firm in center. Remove from oven. Let stand 10 minutes in a warm place. Loosen edges with a spatula; unmold onto warm platter. Makes 4 to 6 servings.

❀ Savory Salmon-Tuna Loaf

1 (7 oz.) can chunk-style
  tuna
1 (7¾ oz.) can salmon
2 tablespoons butter or
  margarine
2 tablespoons chopped
  onion
1 cup soft white bread
  crumbs

2 eggs
¾ cup milk
2 tablespoons chopped
  parsley
½ teaspoon salt
½ teaspoon Worcestershire
  sauce
1 tablespoon lemon juice

SAUCE:

1 (1 lb.) can stewed
  tomatoes, with liquid

1 tablespoon cornstarch

Preheat oven to 350°. Grease a 9 by 5 by 3 inch loaf pan. Place a lightly greased strip of foil down center, letting it extend over ends. Drain tuna. Drain salmon; remove skin and bones. In hot butter in small skillet sauté onion until tender. Stir in bread crumbs. Remove from heat. In medium bowl beat eggs slightly. Stir in milk, parsley, salt, Worcestershire, and bread-crumb mixture. Fold in tuna, salmon, and lemon juice until well blended. Turn into prepared loaf pan. Bake 45 minutes, or until knife inserted in center comes out clean.

SAUCE: Drain ¼ cup liquid from tomatoes into small saucepan.

Stir in cornstarch until dissolved; stir in tomatoes and remaining liquid. Bring to boil, stirring constantly. Keep warm.

Let loaf stand about 3 minutes. Loosen around edges with spatula; holding foil, gently lift loaf onto serving platter so brown crust is on top. Carefully remove foil. Serve loaf with sauce. Makes 6 servings.

❀ Scalloped Salmon

1⅓ cups packaged seasoned bread dressing

⅓ cup melted butter or margarine

1 (1 lb.) can salmon

3 hard-cooked eggs, chopped

1 can condensed cream of mushroom soup

1 tablespoon instant minced onion

1 tablespoon dried parsley flakes

Heat oven to 400°. Combine bread dressing and butter; set aside ⅓ cup of the mixture. Drain salmon, reserving liquid; add enough water to salmon liquid to make ¾ cup. Combine the 1 cup crumb mixture with the salmon, salmon liquid, eggs, soup, onion, and parsley flakes. Place in a shallow, greased 1-quart baking dish and sprinkle with reserved crumbs. Bake 20 minutes. Makes 6 servings.

❀ Scallops with Tartare Sauce

TARTARE SAUCE:

½ cup mayonnaise or cooked salad dressing

2 tablespoons sweet pickle relish

1 tablespoon chopped capers

1 teaspoon prepared mustard

SCALLOPS:

1 egg

½ teaspoon seasoned salt

⅛ teaspoon garlic powder

1 pound sea scallops, washed and drained well

½ cup packaged dry bread crumbs

salad oil or shortening for frying

TARTARE SAUCE: In small bowl combine mayonnaise with pickle

relish, capers, and mustard; mix well. Refrigerate until well chilled
—at least 2 hours.

SCALLOPS: In deep skillet heat salad oil (at least 1 inch) to 375°
on deep-frying thermometer. In small bowl beat egg with seasoned salt and garlic powder. Dip scallops in egg mixture; roll in
crumbs, coating evenly. Fry, a few at a time, until golden brown—
2 to 3 minutes. Drain on paper towels; keep warm while frying rest.
Serve with Tartare Sauce and lemon wedges, if desired. Makes 3
servings.

❀ Seafarer's Spaghetti

1 medium onion, chopped	½ teaspoon oregano
1 clove garlic, minced	⅛ teaspoon pepper
3 tablespoons salad oil	1 (6½ or 7 oz.) can tuna,
2 (8 oz.) cans tomato sauce	drained, or 1 (7½ oz.) can
1 cup water	minced clams, drained
¼ cup chopped fresh	8 ounces spaghetti, cooked
parsley	and drained
1 teaspoon salt	

Cook onion with garlic in salad oil until tender. Add tomato sauce,
water, parsley, and seasonings; simmer 30 minutes. Add tuna or
clams; simmer 5 minutes more. Serve over hot cooked spaghetti.
Makes 3 servings.

❀ Shrimp con Riso

1½ pounds shrimp	2 cups canned tomatoes
salted water	½ teaspoon basil
1 tablespoon salad oil	½ teaspoon salt
⅓ cup thinly sliced onion	pepper
½ cup diced celery	2½ cups hot cooked rice

Cook shrimp in simmering salted water about 5 minutes, or until
pink; do not boil. Heat oil in saucepan over low heat; add onion and
celery and cook until tender, stirring occasionally. Add tomatoes,
basil, salt, and pepper; cook over low heat 20 minutes. Add shrimp
and heat 5 minutes. Serve over rice. Makes 4 servings.

❀ *Shrimp Gumbo*

1 tablespoon cornstarch
1 (1 lb.) can stewed
    tomatoes
¼ cup chili sauce
1 teaspoon Worcestershire
    sauce
liquid hot-pepper seasoning
½ teaspoon seasoned salt

¼ teaspoon dried thyme
1 (8 oz.) can cut okra,
    with liquid
1 (7 oz.) package frozen
    shelled, deveined shrimp,
    thawed
1 cup hot cooked rice

In medium saucepan blend cornstarch with some of liquid from
tomatoes. Stir in tomatoes, chili sauce, Worcestershire, few drops
hot-pepper seasoning, salt, and thyme. Bring to boil, reduce heat,
and simmer 10 minutes. Add okra and shrimp; simmer 5 minutes
longer. Serve over rice. Makes 2 to 6 servings.

❀ *Southern-Style Fish Fillets*

1 cup sliced celery
¼ cup chopped onion
2 tablespoons salad oil
1 pound fish fillets
1 (8 oz.) can tomato sauce

2 tablespoons lemon juice
1 tablespoon Worcestershire
    sauce
1 teaspoon salt

Lightly cook celery and onion in salad oil; add fillets and cook until
golden. Add remaining ingredients. Cover; simmer 10 minutes, or
until fish is done. Makes 3 servings.

❀ *Stuffed Tuna Buns*

1 (7 oz.) can tuna, drained
¼ pound Cheddar cheese,
    cut into ½-inch cubes
3 hard-cooked eggs,
    chopped
1 tablespoon green pepper,
    minced
3 tablespoons onion,
    minced

¼ cup sliced stuffed olives
2 tablespoons pickle relish
¼ teaspoon salt
1 (8 oz.) can tomato sauce
6 buns or rolls
butter

Combine all ingredients except buns and butter. Split buns; spread with butter. Spoon filling between bun halves. Wrap each sandwich in aluminum foil. Bake at 325° for 20 minutes. Makes 6 servings.

❀ *Tuna Biscuit Lace-Up*

1 (*12 oz.*) *can chunk light
   tuna, drained*
1 *cup diced Cheddar or
   mild process cheese*
1 *cup cooked peas*
½ *cup mayonnaise*
¼ *cup chopped onion*

1 *teaspoon salt*
¼ *teaspoon pepper*
2½ *cups packaged biscuit
   mix*
⅔ *cup milk*
⅓ *cup salad oil*

Combine tuna, cheese, peas, mayonnaise, onion, salt, and pepper. Place biscuit mix in mixing bowl; pour milk and salad oil into measuring cup. Pour all at once into biscuit mix and mix well. Turn out on lightly floured surface; knead lightly about 10 times. Roll to 15 by 12 inch rectangle. Starting from one narrow end, spoon tuna mixture down rectangle in strip about 4 inches wide. Cut slashes in dough at 1-inch intervals on both sides of tuna; bring up strips of dough and lace over top, sealing ends securely. Bake at 425° for 25 to 30 minutes. Makes 6 servings.

❀ *Tuna Cornucopias*

2 *cups all-purpose baking
   mix*
4 *tablespoons salad oil*
2 (*8 oz.*) *cans tomato sauce*
½ *teaspoon curry powder*
1 (*7 oz.*) *can tuna, drained*

1 (*8½ oz.*) *can peas, drained*
1 *cup shredded Cheddar
   cheese*
2 *tablespoons mayonnaise*
2 *tablespoons minced onion*

Combine baking mix as for biscuit dough with oil, ⅔ cup tomato sauce, and curry powder. Knead lightly on a floured surface; roll out ¼ inch thick; cut into 6 (4-inch) rounds. Meanwhile, combine tuna with ½ cup peas, ½ cup cheese, mayonnaise, and onion. Spoon tuna mixture in equal amounts on dough rounds; dampen edges; fold over one half of dough to form cornucopia shape, pinch to seal. Arrange on a lightly oiled foil-covered cake rack; place on cookie sheet. Bake at 400° 15 to 20 minutes. Combine remaining tomato sauce, peas, and cheese; heat, stirring. Serve over cornucopias. Makes 4 servings.

❀ *Tuna Dinner Pancakes*

*1 cup commercial sour
  cream*
1 (8 oz.) can tomato sauce
1 (7 oz.) can tuna, drained
*¼ cup chopped green
  pepper*
*¼ cup chopped canned
  pimiento*

1¼ cups pancake mix
1 cup milk
1 egg
*1 cup grated Cheddar
  cheese*

Combine first 5 ingredients thoroughly. Heat slowly; don't boil. Mix together pancake mix, milk, and egg. Make 4 large pancakes on lightly greased hot griddle. Fill each pancake with tuna mixture, roll up, and place in shallow baking dish. Sprinkle with grated cheese. Place under broiler until cheese melts. Makes 4 servings.

❀ *Tuna-Rice Pie*

2 cups cooked rice
1 egg, beaten
2 tablespoons butter
*1 (6½ oz.) can tuna,
  drained*
*1 cup shredded Cheddar
  cheese*
¼ cup chopped celery

¼ cup finely chopped onion
3 eggs
*1 (8 oz.) can tomato sauce
  with mushrooms*
*1 tablespoon chopped
  parsley*
½ teaspoon salt
¼ teaspoon pepper

Combine rice, egg, and butter. Line a buttered 9-inch pie plate with rice mixture. Bake at 400° for 8 minutes. Spread tuna and shredded cheese evenly over rice shell. Combine remaining ingredients and pour over tuna and cheese. Bake at 325° for 1 hour, or until set. Makes 4 servings.

🏵 Tuna Tetrazzini

7 tablespoons butter or
  margarine
½ pound mushrooms, sliced
½ (1 lb.) package large
  shell macaroni
¼ cup unsifted all-purpose
  flour
1 teaspoon salt

½ teaspoon dry mustard
⅛ teaspoon pepper
2 cups milk
½ cup dry sherry
1 (8 oz.) package sharp
  Cheddar cheese, grated
3 (7 oz.) cans tuna, drained

Preheat oven to 375°. In 3 tablespoons hot butter in medium skillet
sauté mushrooms, stirring occasionally. Cook macaroni as package
directs; drain. Melt remaining butter in medium saucepan. Remove
from heat. Stir in flour, salt, mustard, pepper. Gradually stir in milk
and sherry. Bring to boil, stirring. Remove from heat. Add 1½ cups
cheese, stir until melted. In a 2-quart casserole combine tuna, mushrooms, macaroni, and cheese sauce. Sprinkle remaining cheese over
top. Bake, uncovered, 20 to 25 minutes, or until golden and bubbly.
Makes 6 to 8 servings.

🏵 Zucchini Tuna

1 tablespoon butter
½ cup chopped onion
1 clove garlic, minced
4 medium zucchini, thinly
  sliced
1 (8 oz.) can tomato sauce
1 (7 oz.) can tuna, drained
  and flaked

¼ cup water
1 tablespoon chopped
  parsley
½ teaspoon sugar
⅛ teaspoon thyme
1 cup crumbled soft bread

Sauté onions and garlic in butter in skillet; place zucchini slices on
top. Combine tomato sauce, tuna, water, parsley, sugar, and thyme;
mix well. Pour tuna mixture over zucchini slices. Simmer, covered,
for 20 minutes. Uncover, add soft bread, and cook until zucchini
is tender. Sprinkle with Parmesan cheese, if desired. Makes 4 to 5
servings.

EGGS AND CHEESE

In many homes it is easy to know when it's just before pay day—omelets and Welsh rarebit appear as main dishes at mealtime. There's certainly nothing wrong with this. Egg and cheese dishes are not only economical but they are good substitutes for meat since each is high in protein.

Let's take a look first at eggs, to see how they can help the budget-watcher husband her resources. (Odd how that word *husband* used as a verb means to manage frugally, when as a noun it can stir up visions of extravagance!) The protein, vitamins, and minerals contained in eggs are needed for growth; they help maintain strong bodies. Which is one reason why eggs in some form are recommended for regular use in the diet. Eggs are low in calories, of course, and so they are a favorite of the dieter as well as being an excellent food for all the family. This means that the homemaker is going to be buying eggs every time she does her weekly shopping. But standing in front of the dairy counter looking at the various egg signs can be more than a little puzzling.

There are large eggs, medium eggs, and small eggs; brown eggs and white eggs; signs talk about Grade AA, A, B, and C eggs. The first thing to master is color. An egg is an egg whether its shell is brown or white. Eggs with brown shells taste as good and have the same nutritional value as those with white shells. It's all a matter of personal preference—or tradition. If your mother always bought white eggs, chances are you will. Just make sure family loyalties aren't costing you pennies more per dozen. In some areas white eggs are higher priced than brown; in others it's vice versa.

Remember that with eggs it is size, not color, that counts. Small and Medium eggs sometimes sell for as much as one fourth less than the Large and Extra-Large size in the same grade. Grades, of course, refer to egg quality. There are Grade A Extra Large, Large, Medium, Small, and Grade B Extra Large, Large, Medium, Small, and so on.

For really fine price comparisons you need to know weights. Jumbo eggs must weigh at least 30 ounces to the dozen. Each other size—Extra Large, Large, Medium, and Small—is three ounces less, down to Very Small, which weigh only 15 ounces to the dozen. Figuring the price per ounce will let you know when it is wiser to buy eggs of one grade and size over another.

It is far simpler, however, to base your selection on use. Top grade eggs (AA or A) are worth the extra price. They taste and look better if you are going to fry, poach, or cook them in the shell. Grade B eggs are equally desirable for baking and cooking purposes as well as for scrambling. There's no need to spend money on the best grades when lesser ones will do. Just make certain you buy from a refrigerated case and refrigerate the eggs promptly at home, keeping the large end of the eggs up. (We don't know whether it was a chicken who revealed the secret or not, but this trick keeps the yolks better centered in the whites.)

By scanning all the weekend ads, you are bound to find at least one special on eggs that will save you at least 10 percent. It is a fact of supermarketry that bargain eggs will draw customers.

Cheese is one of man's finest inventions. Nutritionally it is one of the most perfect of foods, providing the same vitamins and minerals as milk but in condensed form. As an aid to ailing budgets, it performs nobly: as little as ¼ to ½ pound of firm cheese (1 to 1½ cups grated) will make a macaroni and cheese casserole or a soufflé to serve four. Few food friends in your kitchen can make that boast.

Nobody has ever been able to count the different cheeses in the world. The U. S. Department of Agriculture has figured out a compressed list of 18 basic types of cheese, and under each type there are at least 20 different varieties. No wonder most homemakers are familiar with the temptation that awaits them in a cheese store or at a cheese counter—how to depart with just one variety?

Perhaps lesson No. 1 in making cheese fit into your budgetary plan is to be firm as a good Gruyère and buy only as much cheese as you need for a specific menu or can consume within a month. Soft dessert cheeses dry up or get strong in a short time, even when refrigerated. Semisoft cheese lasts a little longer, and semifirm will still be tasty in two months or more, if properly wrapped.

Most homemakers are aware of the four major cheese divisions— Soft (Brie, Camembert, Cottage, Cream, etc.), Semisoft (Bel Paese, Monterey, Mozzarella, Munster, etc.), Firm to Hard (Cheddar, Edam, Provolone, Swiss, etc.), and Hard (Parmesan and Romano types, usually grated).

Much less expensive than the natural cheeses, of course, are the process cheeses. A blend of cheeses heated to a very high temperature and combined in many instances with artificial stabilizers, process cheeses are apt to have a bland, innocuous flavor. They do keep for long periods if tightly wrapped.

One obvious way to save money when buying cheese is to stay away from the individually wrapped slices. Convenient, yes. Cheaper, no. Cut your cheese slices yourself; it is far less expensive. And, delightful as they may be for cocktail snacks, those crocks of ready-to-serve cheese spreads, such as Cheddar with Port or Edam with Sauterne, are far from a thrifty buy. Make up your own combinations, using leftover cheeses that are beginning to dry up. Also, grate those leftover odds and ends to enrich vegetable entrees or to perk up salads and soups.

Cheese should be kept refrigerated but always served at room temperature, which allows the full flavor to release. Don't attempt to keep soft cheeses, such as cottage and cream cheese, too long after purchase, since they are quite perishable. Hard cheeses may be frozen, but freezing may change the characteristic body and texture and cause the cheese to become crumbly and mealy.

If you really want to economize in the cheese department, the best way to do it is to keep alert for dairy counter specials. Don't attempt to make cheese yourself, at least not following Mrs. E. Smith's recipe. That frugal soul, in a book called *The Compleat Housewife,* written in 1742, began her recipe for Cheddar: "Take the new milk of 12 cows in the morning and the evening cream of 12 cows and put to it three spoonfuls of rennet . . . and work into the curd three pounds of fresh butter . . ."

❁ Baked Deviled Eggs

2 (8 oz.) cans tomato sauce
2 tablespoons brown sugar
1 tablespoon chopped onion
¼ teaspoon powdered
  thyme
6 hard-cooked eggs

1 tablespoon mayonnaise
1 teaspoon vinegar
½ teaspoon prepared
  mustard
½ teaspoon salt
⅛ teaspoon pepper

Pour tomato sauce into 6 by 10 by 2 inch baking dish, reserving 2 tablespoons. Add brown sugar, onion, and thyme to sauce; mix well. Cut eggs in half lengthwise. Remove yolks and mix them with the two tablespoons tomato sauce and remaining ingredients. Fill egg whites and place in sauce. Bake at 350° for 20 to 25 minutes, or until tops of eggs are lightly browned and sauce bubbles. Serve on hot buttered rice. Makes 3 to 4 servings.

❁ Baked Eggs Gruyère

1 (6 oz.) package indi-
  vidual Gruyère cheese
  wedges
10 crisp cooked bacon slices

6 eggs
½ cup heavy cream
⅛ teaspoon pepper

Preheat oven to 350°. Generously butter a 10 by 6 by 2 inch baking dish. Cut each of 5 cheese wedges lengthwise into fourths. Cover bottom of prepared dish with cheese slices. Crumble bacon over cheese in dish. Carefully break eggs over cheese and bacon. Spoon cream over eggs; sprinkle with pepper. Grate remaining cheese wedge and sprinkle over eggs. Bake, uncovered, 20 minutes, or just until eggs are set. Makes 3 to 4 servings.

❁ Crunchy Baked Eggs

6 bacon slices, diced
2 cups corn flakes, crushed
8 eggs
salt

pepper
4 teaspoons grated
  Parmesan cheese

Preheat oven at 375°. Grease 4 (10 oz.) custard cups. In medium skillet sauté bacon until crisp. Remove from skillet and drain on paper towels. Pour off bacon drippings; return 2 tablespoons to skillet. Add corn flakes to skillet, toss to coat with drippings. Sprinkle about 1 tablespoon·bacon in bottom of each prepared custard cup. With back of spoon, press corn-flake mixture against sides of cup around bacon to form a nest, using about ½ cup for each nest. Gently slip eggs (2 at a time) into nests. Sprinkle with salt and pepper. Bake 10 minutes. Sprinkle with cheese; bake 5 to 7 minutes longer, or until of desired doneness. Makes 4 servings.

🏵 *Eggs Fu Yung*

1 teaspoon soy sauce
1 teaspoon dark molasses
1 teaspoon cider vinegar
2 teaspoons cornstarch
½ cup canned chicken
  broth, undiluted
1 cup finely chopped
  cooked ham or pork

1 cup canned bean sprouts,
  drained
1 cup finely chopped onion
6 eggs, slightly beaten
1 teaspoon salt
1 tablespoon soy sauce
salad oil

In top of double boiler combine 1 teaspoon soy sauce, molasses, vinegar, and cornstarch, stirring until smooth. Gradually stir in chicken broth; over direct heat bring to boil, stirring. Reduce heat and simmer 10 minutes. Sauce will be thickened and translucent. Keep warm over hot water. In large bowl, combine ham, bean sprouts, and onion. Add eggs, salt, and 1 tablespoon soy sauce, stirring until combined. Slowly heat a little oil in small skillet. Add egg mixture about 2 tablespoons at a time (as for pancakes). Sauté, turning once, until just browned on both sides. Remove and keep warm. Repeat until all egg mixture is used. Arrange "pancakes" on hot platter. Pour hot sauce over them. Makes 4 to 6 servings.

❁ *French Omelet with Chicken Livers*

4 slices bacon
½ pound chicken livers
½ cup chopped onion
½ cup coarsely chopped
   green pepper

½ teaspoon salt
½ teaspoon Worcestershire
   sauce
¼ cup water

OMELET:

6 eggs
3 tablespoons water
½ teaspoon salt

2 tablespoons butter or
   margarine

In skillet fry bacon until crisp. Drain on paper towels; crumble. Add chicken livers to bacon drippings in skillet; sauté 3 to 4 minutes. Remove with slotted utensil to board; chop coarsely. Add onion and green pepper to skillet; sauté until tender—about 5 minutes. Add chicken liver, bacon, salt, Worcestershire, and water; heat gently. Cover and keep warm.

OMELET: In medium bowl with rotary beater beat eggs with the water and salt until well blended but not frothy. Slowly heat a 10-inch heavy skillet. Add butter and heat until it sizzles briskly. Turn egg mixture into skillet; cook over medium heat. As egg sets, run spatula around edge to loosen, and tilt pan to let uncooked portion run underneath. Continue loosening and tilting until omelet is almost dry on top and golden brown underneath. Place chicken-liver mixture in center. Fold omelet in half and slide onto heated serving plate. Makes 4 servings.

❁ *Hangtown Scramble*

6 slices bacon, cut in
   ½-inch pieces
1 (8 oz.) can oysters, well
   drained (clams or shrimp
   may be substituted)
½ cup cracker crumbs
3 tablespoons chopped
   green onions

6 eggs
⅓ cup milk
½ teaspoon salt
dash pepper
1 (8 oz.) can tomato sauce

Fry diced bacon in skillet. Coat oysters with cracker crumbs. Add oysters and green onions and sauté in bacon fat. Combine eggs, milk, salt, and pepper; pour over bacon-oyster mixture. Cover and cook slowly until eggs are set. Pour tomato sauce over. Cover and heat through. Makes 4 servings.

❀ Mushroom Scrambled Eggs

6 eggs
1 tablespoon instant-type
  flour
½ teaspoon salt
dash pepper
⅓ cup light cream

1 tablespoon dry sherry
2 tablespoons butter or
  margarine
1 (3 oz.) can sliced mushrooms, drained
2 green onions, sliced

In large bowl with rotary beater, beat eggs until frothy. Sprinkle with flour, salt, and pepper; beat until smooth. Beat in cream and sherry. Melt butter in 9-inch skillet over medium heat. Pour egg mixture into skillet; cook slowly. As eggs start to set, gently lift cooked portion with spatula, to let uncooked portion flow to bottom of skillet. Add mushrooms. When eggs are cooked but still shiny and moist, remove from heat. Turn into serving dish. Sprinkle with onions. Serve with toast slices. Makes 3 to 4 servings.

❀ Onion-Potato Frittata

2 tablespoons butter or
  margarine
⅓ cup thinly sliced onion
1 cup diced, pared raw
  potato
6 eggs

2 tablespoons water
1 teaspoon seasoned salt
dash dried thyme leaves
1 tablespoon finely chopped
  parsley

Slowly melt butter in a 9-inch heavy skillet or omelet pan with heat-resistant handle. Add onion and potato; sauté, stirring, 8 to 10 minutes, or until potato is tender. Meanwhile, with rotary beater, beat eggs with water, salt, thyme, and parsley until combined, not frothy. Pour egg mixture over onion and potato. Cook over low heat. As eggs set, lift with spatula to let uncooked portion run underneath. When eggs are almost set on top, run under broiler, 6 inches from heat, 2 to 3 minutes, or until golden. Turn out, without folding, onto heated serving platter. Makes 3 to 4 servings.

❊ Sausage and Eggs Creole

½ pound pork sausage links,   8 eggs
  cut in 1-inch pieces   ½ cup milk
2 (8 oz.) cans tomato sauce   ¼ teaspoon salt
½ cup finely chopped green · dash pepper
  pepper   buttered toast
2 tablespoons instant   commercial sour cream
  minced onion

Brown sausage links in saucepan; pour off excess fat. Add tomato sauce, green pepper, and onion. Simmer 5 minutes. Beat together eggs, milk, salt, and pepper. Scramble in buttered skillet. Place servings of scrambled eggs on buttered toast. Spoon on sausage-tomato sauce and top with dollops of sour cream. Makes 4 to 5 servings.

❊ Scrambled Eggs à la Suisse

8 eggs   2 tablespoons butter or
½ cup light cream   margarine
½ teaspoon salt   snipped chives or parsley
dash cayenne pepper
1 cup grated natural Swiss
  cheese (¼ lb.)

With rotary beater beat eggs, cream, salt, and cayenne in top of double boiler until well combined. Stir in ¾ cup Swiss cheese and the butter. Cook over gently boiling water, stirring occasionally, 12 to 15 minutes, or until eggs are set but still creamy. Serve eggs sprinkled with rest of cheese and the chives or parsley. Makes 4 to 6 servings.

✿ Spinach-Sour Cream Omelet

FILLING:

1 (10 oz.) package frozen   ½ teaspoon salt
  chopped spinach   ⅛ teaspoon nutmeg
⅓ cup commercial sour
  cream

OMELET:

6 eggs   1½ tablespoons butter or
½ teaspoon salt   margarine
dash pepper   sour cream
1 tablespoon cold water

FILLING: Cook spinach as package label directs; drain well. Add
⅓ cup sour cream, the salt, and nutmeg. Cover and keep warm.

OMELET: In medium bowl, with wire whisk or rotary beater, beat
eggs, salt, pepper, and cold water until just combined but not
frothy. Meanwhile, slowly heat 9-inch skillet or omelet pan. Add
butter; heat until it sizzles briskly—it should not brown. Turn
omelet mixture all at once into skillet; cook over medium heat. As
omelet sets, run spatula around edge to loosen; tilt pan to let uncooked portion run underneath. Continue loosening and tilting until omelet is almost dry on top and golden brown underneath. Spoon
warm filling down center of omelet; fold in half. Tilt out onto heated
platter. Top with additional sour cream, if desired. Makes 4 servings.

✿ Tuna Soufflé

¼ cup butter or margarine   dash of ground turmeric
¼ cup chopped onion   1 tablespoon lemon juice
¼ cup flour   1 tablespoon chopped
1 cup milk   parsley
½ cup shredded sharp   5 eggs, separated (at room
  Cheddar cheese   temperature)
½ teaspoon Worcestershire   2 (6½ or 7 oz.) cans tuna,
¼ teaspoon salt   well drained and finely
¼ teaspoon dry mustard   flaked
dash of cayenne pepper

Heat oven to 350°. Melt butter in a saucepan over moderately low heat; add onion and cook until tender. Quickly stir in flour and blend until smooth. Heat until bubbly. Remove from heat and gradually add milk, stirring constantly. Return to heat and bring to a boil, stirring constantly; boil 1 minute longer, stirring constantly. Add cheese, Worcestershire, salt, mustard, cayenne, and turmeric. Cook and stir until cheese melts. Remove from heat and stir in lemon juice and parsley. In a large bowl beat egg yolks slightly. Gradually stir in cheese mixture. Stir in tuna. Beat egg whites until stiff but not dry. Fold into tuna mixture. Turn into 2-quart soufflé dish. Bake 45 minutes. Serve immediately. Makes 4 to 6 servings.

✿ *Bacon 'n Tomato Rarebit*

6 *slices bacon*
½ *cup chopped onion*
½ *cup chopped green*
   pepper
¼ *cup flour*
1 *cup milk*
1 *(8 oz.) can tomato sauce*

1 *cup (¼ lb.) shredded*
   sharp process cheese
1 *teaspoon Worcestershire*
   sauce
6 *English muffins, split and*
   toasted

Cook bacon until crisp; drain. Cook onion and green pepper in about 6 tablespoons of the bacon fat until tender. Blend in flour. Stir in milk and tomato sauce; cook until thickened. Add cheese and Worcestershire. Stir until cheese is melted. Serve over toasted English muffins. Top each serving with a strip of cooked bacon. Makes 6 servings.

✿ *Baked Smoky-Cheese Sandwiches*

8 *cheese bread or white*
   bread slices, crusts
   removed
2 *(6 oz.) packages hickory-*
   smoke-flavor cheese
3 *eggs*

2 *cups milk*
1 *tablespoon prepared*
   mustard
1 *teaspoon salt*
⅛ *teaspoon pepper*
paprika

Make 4 sandwiches, using the bread and cheese. Place in a single layer in an 8 by 8 by 2 inch baking dish. In medium bowl with rotary beater beat together eggs, milk, mustard, salt, and pepper. Pour over sandwiches, covering completely. Refrigerate, covered, several hours; turn several times. Preheat oven to 350°. Sprinkle sandwiches with paprika. Bake 50 minutes or until they are golden brown and cheese is melted. Makes 4 servings.

❀ *Cheese and Macaroni Bake*

1 (8 oz.) package elbow macaroni	1 cup Ricotta or cottage cheese
1 tablespoon salad oil	1 cup commercial sour cream
2 tablespoons minced onion	
½ teaspoon salt	1 (8 oz.) can tomato sauce
¼ teaspoon garlic powder	

Cook macaroni according to package directions. Drain. Cook onion in salad oil until tender. Combine all ingredients. Toss lightly. Spoon into 2-quart casserole and bake at 350° for 30 minutes. Makes 4 servings.

❀ *Cheese-Lined Burgers*

1 pound ground beef	4 slices sharp cheese
salt	1 (8 oz.) can tomato sauce
pepper	

Form beef into 8 very thin patties. Sprinkle with salt and pepper. Place cheese on 4 patties; cover with remaining patties. Pinch edges together to enclose the cheese completely. Brown on one side in hot skillet; turn and pour over tomato sauce. Simmer 8 to 10 minutes, basting occasionally. Makes 4 servings.

❀ *Cheese-Noodle Casserole*

8 ounces medium-wide noodles	1 tablespoon grated onion
	¼ teaspoon Tabasco
1 cup large-curd cottage cheese	2 tablespoons chopped pimiento
1 teaspoon Worcestershire sauce	1 tablespoon chopped green pepper
½ teaspoon salt	½ cup shredded sharp Cheddar cheese
1 cup commercial sour cream	

Heat oven to 350°. Cook noodles in boiling salted water as package directs. Drain. Combine noodles, cottage cheese, Worcestershire, salt, sour cream, onion, Tabasco, pimiento, and green pepper. Turn into buttered 2-quart casserole. Sprinkle top with Cheddar cheese. Bake 25 to 30 minutes, until thoroughly heated and top is brown. Makes 4 servings.

✿ *Cheese-Potato Soufflé*

1 (4 serving) package instant mashed potatoes	⅛ teaspoon cayenne pepper
4 eggs, separated	1 can condensed cream of
8 ounces sharp Cheddar cheese, grated	mushroom soup, undiluted
1 teaspoon Worcestershire sauce	1 cup commercial sour cream
½ teaspoon salt	

Heat oven to 350°. Prepare mashed potatoes according to package directions. Add slightly beaten egg yolks, cheese, Worcestershire, salt, and cayenne pepper. Beat egg whites until stiff but not dry; fold into potato mixture. Bake in a greased 1½-quart casserole 50 to 60 minutes, until crust is deep golden brown. Combine cream of mushroom soup and sour cream. Heat and serve over soufflé. Makes 4 servings.

✿ *Five-Way Pizzas*

1 package refrigerator biscuits	¼ teaspoon basil
	shredded Mozzarella cheese
1 (8 oz.) can tomato sauce with cheese	sliced salami, cooked pork
1 tablespoon salad oil	sausage, sliced wieners,
1 tablespoon minced onion	smoked cocktail sausages,
½ teaspoon oregano	Vienna sausages

Separate biscuit dough and roll each biscuit into ⅛-inch-thick rounds on lightly floured surface. Place on ungreased cookie sheet. Spread with sauce made from mixture of tomato sauce, salad oil, onion, oregano, and basil heated together. Sprinkle with Mozzarella. Top with any or all of the 5 suggested toppings. Bake at 400° for 10 to 15 minutes, or until crust is golden brown. Makes 4 servings.

❀ French Toasted Sandwiches

8 slices bacon
8 slices bread
8 slices process American
  cheese

4 tablespoons butter or
  margarine
2 eggs, beaten
⅓ cup milk

Cook bacon in small skillet over low heat. Drain on paper towels.
On half the bread slices arrange 2 slices cooked bacon and 2 slices
cheese per slice. Top with rest of bread. Cut each sandwich in half.
Melt butter in large skillet over low heat. Combine eggs and milk.
Dip sandwiches carefully in egg mixture. Brown on both sides over
low heat. Makes 4 full sandwiches.

❀ Macaroni-Cheese Twist

½ green pepper, diced
1 clove garlic, minced
1 medium onion, chopped
  fine
1 tablespoon salad oil
2 (8 oz.) cans tomato sauce
1 cup water
½ teaspoon oregano
2 tablespoons finely
  chopped parsley

4 ounces process American
  cheese, cut in ½-inch
  cubes
8 ounces corkscrew
  macaroni, cooked and
  drained

In skillet cook green pepper, onion and garlic in oil until tender.
Stir in tomato sauce, water, oregano, and parsley; simmer 10 minutes. Add cheese cubes; stir just to mix. Serve immediately over hot
macaroni. Makes 4 servings.

❁ Olive-Cheese Loaf

8 ounce package of
   macaroni, cooked and
   drained
1½ cups milk
2 tablespoons salad oil
2 cups shredded sharp
   Cheddar cheese
½ cup soft bread crumbs

2 eggs, well beaten
⅓ cup sliced stuffed olives
2 tablespoons minced
   parsley
1 tablespoon instant minced
   onion
2 teaspoons salt
¼ teaspoon pepper

Combine all ingredients. Pour into greased 9 by 5 by 3 inch loaf pan. Bake at 325° for 30 to 35 minutes. Makes 4 servings.

❁ Pizza Spaghetti

½ cup chopped onion
1 clove garlic, minced
2 tablespoons salad oil
2 (8 oz.) cans tomato sauce
   with mushrooms
¼ cup water
1 teaspoon basil
1 teaspoon oregano
½ teaspoon salt

8 ounces spaghetti, broken,
   cooked, and drained
1 cup shredded Mozzarella,
   Swiss, or mild process
   cheese
sliced salami or pepperoni,
   cooked link sausages,
   olives and/or green
   pepper strips

In skillet lightly cook onion and garlic in oil. Stir in tomato sauce, water, basil, oregano, and salt. Simmer, covered, 15 minutes. Place spaghetti on an oven-proof platter; spoon tomato sauce mixture over and mix gently. Sprinkle with cheese, then arrange any or all of the suggested toppings over the cheese, pizza style. Bake at 350° for 5 minutes, or until cheese melts. Makes 4 servings.

❀ Spaghetti Ring

8 ounces spaghetti, cooked
  and drained
1 cup cottage cheese
½ cup grated Parmesan
  cheese
2 eggs, slightly beaten
1½ teaspoons salt
⅛ teaspoon pepper
1 tablespoon instant minced
  onion

1 (8 oz.) can tomato sauce
2 tablespoons salad oil
2 tablespoons flour
1½ cups milk
½ teaspoon salt
⅛ teaspoon pepper
⅛ teaspoon oregano or
  thyme
1 (10 oz.) package frozen
  mixed vegetables, cooked

Line 9-inch ring mold with aluminum foil; grease foil. Mix spaghetti, cottage cheese, Parmesan cheese, eggs, salt, pepper, onion, and ½ can tomato sauce; pack in ring mold. Bake at 350° for 35 to 40 minutes. While ring is baking, make cream sauce with salad oil, flour, and milk. Stir in salt, pepper, oregano, mixed vegetables, and remaining ½ can tomato sauce. Heat and serve in center of unmolded spaghetti ring. Makes 4 servings.

❀ Swiss Cheese Fondue

1 clove garlic, split
1 pound natural Swiss
  cheese, grated
1¼ cups dry white wine
dash salt

dash pepper
2 tablespoons cornstarch
1 long loaf French or Italian
  bread

For fondue use a fondue pot, deep baking dish with glazed interior, flame-proof glass saucepan, or crockery utensil; never use a metal pan. Rub bottom and side of fondue pot with cut sides of garlic. Place cheese, 1 cup wine, salt, and pepper in pot. Cook over medium heat, stirring constantly, until cheese melts. Remove from heat. (Do not cook longer, even though cheese and wine are not blended.) In small bowl, make a smooth paste of cornstarch and remaining wine. With wire whisk, mix the cornstarch mixture into the cheese mixture. Return to medium heat; cook, stirring constantly, 2 to 3 minutes, or until fondue is creamy and as thick as medium white sauce. To serve, set fondue over low flame or candle warmer. Cut bread into 1-inch cubes for dipping into fondue. Makes 12 servings.

❀ *Tomato Fondue*

3 eggs, slightly beaten
2 (8 oz.) cans tomato sauce
1 cup milk
1 tablespoon chopped
   parsley
1 teaspoon basil

1 teaspoon salt
¼ teaspoon pepper
8 slices day-old bread
½ pound shredded sharp
   Cheddar cheese

Heat oven to 325°. Combine eggs, tomato sauce, milk, parsley, basil, salt, and pepper. Arrange alternate layers of bread slices, egg mixture, and cheese in a shallow, greased 2-quart casserole. Place casserole in a pan containing ½ inch hot water. Bake 50 minutes, until a knife inserted in the center comes out clean. Makes 4 servings.

VEGETABLES

Decisions, decisions, decisions.

They are what you have to make when you're out to save money on vegetables. Keeping in mind the menus you are planning, you must decide what type of vegetable will do the best and cheapest job for you. Fresh? Washed, trimmed, and packaged? Frozen? Dehydrated? Canned? And if canned, premium pack or one of the less choice grades? Name brand or private label?

It's no simple matter to be a budget-watcher!

A recent survey on the cost of potatoes is a convincing example of how one can save money by considering all forms of a vegetable. Conducted in New York State, the study revealed that the cost per serving of fresh potatoes was 2 cents; dehydrated mashed, between 3 and 4 cents; frozen whipped, about 5 cents; canned, 6 cents; dehydrated au gratin and frozen French-fried, about 8 cents; frozen stuffed, about 11 cents.

Obviously, fresh vegetables can be your best buy when they are in season and plentiful. Vegetables that do not grow in your area year round but must be flown in during winter months are going to cost more. Buy them only when they are in season. Prices decline when local farms can supply your market's needs; at that time they are usually half what they are in winter. Don't rush to buy first-of-the-crop specimens, though; most often their price is high. Wait until the supply increases.

When shopping for fresh vegetables, buy only what you need or can use in short order. Do not buy a lot just because the price is right or you cannot resist their appealing appearance. (What is more beautiful, though, than a basket of rosy red tomatoes or the snowy surface of a cauliflower wreathed in green?) If you buy more than you can properly store in your refrigerator or use without waste, you are simply throwing money away. Most fresh vegetables can be stored for two to five days, except for root vegetables like onions and turnips, which can be stored from one to several weeks.

Pinching pennies is a commendable virtue on the part of a food shopper; pinching fresh vegetables is not. Nonetheless, there is a breed of lady shoppers who can't pick a tomato, avocado, or eggplant without poking and squeezing every one of them in sight. Your problem will be to avoid taking home any of those poor, maltreated specimens. A bruised—or decayed—vegetable will spoil quickly, possibly before you can use it. Sometimes stores put a special on vegetables that are "slightly damaged"—don't succumb. Even if you trim off the decayed area, deterioration will be rapid. Make it your business to buy vegetables that are mature, fresh-looking, and free of bruises, skin punctures, and decay. It is a good investment at all times to spend a few cents extra for vegetables in prime condition. In other words, when it comes to the parsley, don't practice parsimony.

When is it worthwhile to buy pre-washed, trimmed, and packaged vegetables? Normally, only if they are weekend specials and priced lower than usual. Frankly, they are time savers, not money savers. When you buy them, you are paying for service—someone else has cut off the carrot tops, husked the corn, shelled the peas, and done the cleaning. Save money by doing these tasks yourself. You might even get *more* out of a vegetable. Take celery as an example. Packaged celery hearts are fine, but look at what you miss—those upper stalks and green leaves can be a welcome addition to soups, stews, and salads.

There are times when frozen vegetables will be your best buy. For example, just as fresh vegetables come into abundant supply, store managers often mark down their frozen counterparts. Watch for these buys and stock up.

In off season, of course, the frozen vegetable will be less expensive than the hothouse variety or the vegetable shipped in from some distant grower. Frequently, for practical purposes, the frozen vegetable is a wise choice. Frozen peas and spinach are almost always a sensible buy. If you are planning on a creamed-spinach dish, however, don't buy it frozen. It can cost five times as much. Buy the plain frozen spinach and cream it yourself.

If you use only small quantities of a vegetable, the frozen variety

—even at a much higher price per pound—could be a better buy. Frozen chopped geen peppers, onions, parsley, and chives, for example, are a thrifty choice because you can use as much or as little as you wish and save the rest in the freezer. Those large plastic bags of frozen potatoes, carrots, peas, and beans can also be an economical investment.

Canned vegetables are the budget-watcher's mainstay. Here the chief problem is to make the right decision regarding grade. Top grade and premium or fancy packs will obviously cost more than lower grades. Make your choice with use in mind. If you are going to serve tomatoes as a side dish, you'll want the best grade. If they are going to be popped into a casserole or a sauce, a less expensive grade will do.

And here is the place where you must also consider private label versus name brand. Many supermarkets have their own labels, which represent a savings of from 5 to 40 percent. Frequently the two brands are of identical quality because they are packed for retailers by the processors of nationally advertised brands. It is possible, though, that some private-label canned goods may not be up to your own personal standards. But it is worthwhile to try them all and make a choice.

One last thought: if you use a lot of canned vegetables, ask your store manager for a case price. Buying canned goods by the case could mean considerable savings. And you get all those lovely cartons for storing things in or for rainy-day playtime ammunition for the kids.

✿ *Baked Carrots*

3 tablespoons margarine
⅓ cup finely chopped onion
5 cups shredded carrots (about 12 medium carrots)
¾ cup water

1½ teaspoons lemon juice
2 tablespoons light brown sugar
2 teaspoons dry mustard
1 teaspoon salt
3 tablespoons margarine

Heat oven to 350°. Melt 3 tablespoons margarine in a skillet over moderately low heat; add onion and cook until tender, stirring occasionally. Combine onion and carrots in a 1½-quart casserole. Mix together water, lemon juice, brown sugar, mustard, and salt;

stir into carrot mixture. Dot with the remaining 3 tablespoons margarine. Cover and bake 1 hour, or until tender. Makes 8 servings.

❀ *Baked Onion-Corn Casserole*

½ *cup boiling water*
6 *medium onions, peeled*
1 (1 *lb.* 1 *oz.*) *can cream-style corn*
dash ground cloves
¼ *teaspoon turmeric*

½ *teaspoon salt*
¼ *cup packaged dry bread crumbs*
2 *tablespoons melted butter or margarine*

Preheat oven to 375°. In large saucepan, add boiling water to onions; return to boil. Reduce heat; simmer, covered, 20 minutes. Drain onions. Arrange in a 1½-quart casserole. Combine corn, cloves, turmeric, and salt; pour over onions. Toss bread crumbs with butter; sprinkle over vegetables. Bake, uncovered, about 25 minutes, or until top is browned and onions are tender. Makes 6 servings.

❀ *Baked Rice and Vegetables*

2 *tablespoons butter or margarine*
½ *cup uncooked rice*
1 *cup diced carrots*
½ *cup chopped green pepper*
1 (1 *lb.*) *can green beans, drained*

1 *medium onion, thinly sliced*
⅛ *teaspoon salt*
¼ *teaspoon pepper*
1 *chicken bouillon cube*
2 *cups boiling water*

Heat oven to 375°. Melt butter in a skillet over moderate heat. Add rice and brown lightly, stirring frequently. Arrange carrots and green pepper in bottom of a 2-quart casserole. Cover with browned rice. Arrange beans over rice. Spread sliced onion over the top; sprinkle with salt and pepper. Dissolve chicken bouillon cube in the boiling water. Pour over rice and vegetables. Cover. Bake about 1 hour, or until rice and vegetables are tender. Makes 4 servings.

❀ *Beans Creole Style*

1 pound dried lima beans	*2 teaspoons prepared*
6 cups water	*mustard*
½ pound bacon, diced	*1 teaspoon Worcestershire*
1 onion, chopped	*sauce*
1 green pepper, diced	*2 tablespoons brown sugar*
2 teaspoons seasoned salt	*1 (6 oz.) can tomato paste*
¼ teaspoon pepper	*2 cups water*

Cover beans with 6 cups water and let stand overnight. When ready to prepare, cook 1 hour or until tender. Drain. Cook bacon in large skillet until crisp; remove bacon and drain. Add onion and green pepper to bacon fat and cook 5 minutes. Blend in seasonings, tomato paste, and 2 cups water. Simmer 5 minutes; add beans and heat. Sprinkle with bacon. Makes 4 servings.

❀ *Cabbage in Mustard Sauce*

1¼ cups milk	*2 tablespoons flour*
4 cups coarsely shredded	*¼ cup milk*
cabbage	*1 tablespoon butter or*
1½ teaspoons salt	*margarine*
1 teaspoon prepared	
mustard	

Heat 1¼ cups milk in a large saucepan. Add cabbage and salt. Cover loosely and cook over low heat about 5 minutes, or until cabbage is just tender. Stir occasionally. Remove from heat. Do not drain. Measure mustard into small mixing bowl. Gradually blend in flour. Gradually stir in the ¼ cup milk. Add to cabbage; stir gently until well mixed. Add butter. Cook and stir over low heat until thickened. Cook 3 to 4 minutes longer. Makes 4 to 6 servings.

🏵 *Carrot Casserole*

½ *pound young carrots,*   1 *teaspoon dried marjoram*
  sliced   *leaves*
1 (16 oz.) *can tomatoes*   *chopped parsley*
1 *teaspoon salt*
⅛ *teaspoon pepper*

Heat oven to 350°. Combine carrots, tomatoes, salt, pepper, and
marjoram in a lightly greased 1-quart casserole. Bake 45 minutes,
or until carrots are tender. Garnish with chopped parsley. Makes
6 servings.

🏵 *Carrots Vichy*

2½ *tablespoons butter or*   3 *cups scraped, sliced*
  margarine   *carrots*
1 *tablespoon sugar*   ½ *cup boiling water*
¼ *teaspoon salt*   1 *tablespoon chopped*
1½ *teaspoons lemon juice*   *parsley*

Place butter, sugar, salt, and lemon juice in saucepan. Add carrots
and boiling water. Cover. Cook over moderate heat until most of the
water evaporates and carrots are tender. Remove lid. Brown carrots lightly in the butter sauce remaining in pan. Garnish with parsley. Makes 4 servings.

🏵 *Celery au Gratin*

4 *cups 1-inch slices celery*   1 *cup shredded sharp*
2 *tablespoons butter or*   *Cheddar cheese*
  margarine   ½ *teaspoon salt*
2 *tablespoons flour*   ⅛ *teaspoon paprika*
1½ *cups milk*   *few grains cayenne pepper*

Cook celery in small amount of boiling salted water until tender,
about 10 minutes. Drain celery. Melt butter in saucepan over low
heat. Blend in flour; cook until bubbly. Gradually stir in milk. Place
over moderate heat and cook, stirring constantly, until sauce is thickened and smooth. Remove from heat. Add cheese, salt, paprika, and

cayenne pepper. Stir until cheese is melted. Arrange celery in a buttered, shallow 1½-quart baking dish. Pour cheese sauce over celery. Heat oven to 350°. Bake 35 to 40 minutes, or until sauce bubbles. Makes 6 servings.

❈ Cheese Baked Tomatoes

4 medium tomatoes
¾ cup fine dry bread
*   crumbs*

⅓ cup coarsely shredded
*   sharp Cheddar cheese*
¾ cup melted margarine

Heat oven to 375°. Wash tomatoes and cut each in half crosswise. Toss together bread crumbs, cheese, and margarine; mound crumbs on top of tomato halves. Bake 25 to 30 minutes, or until the tomatoes are hot and the bread crumbs on top are lightly browned. Makes 4 to 8 servings.

❈ Fiesta Corn Pudding

2 tablespoons butter or
*   margarine*
2 tablespoons flour
1 cup milk
2 (12 oz.) cans whole
*   kernel corn with sweet*
*   peppers, drained*

2 eggs, separated
¾ teaspoon salt
¼ teaspoon paprika
2 slices crisp cooked bacon,
*   crumbled*

Heat oven to 350°. Melt butter in saucepan over low heat; blend in flour; cook until bubbly. Gradually stir in milk. Cook over moderate heat, stirring constantly, until thickened and smooth. Add corn and bring to a boil. Beat egg yolks. Pour about 1 cup of corn mixture into egg yolks and blend well. Return to corn mixture in saucepan. Cook and stir over moderate heat for a few minutes, until slightly thickened. Add salt, paprika, and bacon. Cool slightly. Beat egg whites until stiff but not dry. Fold into corn mixture. Turn into 1½-quart soufflé dish. Bake about 30 minutes, until set and golden brown on top. Makes 6 servings.

❋ French-Fried Onion Rings

2 *medium Bermuda onions*   1 *teaspoon salt*
  (1½ lbs.)   ¼ *teaspoon baking powder*
salad oil or shortening for   2 *eggs*
  deep-fat frying   1 *cup milk*
1¼ *cups unsifted all-*   1 *tablespoon salad oil*
  purpose flour

Peel onions; slice about ⅓ inch thick; separate into rings. To electric skillet or heavy saucepan over low heat add salad oil to depth of
1 inch and heat to 375° on deep-frying thermometer. Meanwhile,
sift flour, salt, and baking powder. In large bowl with rotary beater
beat eggs slightly. Add milk, 1 tablespoon oil, and the flour mixture; beat just until smooth. With two-tined fork, dip onion rings in
batter (let excess batter drip into bowl). Drop rings, a few at a
time, into hot fat. Fry, turning once, until golden brown. Keep warm
in 200° oven while frying rest. Sprinkle with salt. Makes 8 servings.

❋ Fried Potatoes with Bacon

4 *strips bacon*   1 *teaspoon salt*
4 *large potatoes*   ¼ *teaspoon pepper*

Cook bacon in heavy skillet over moderate heat until crisp. Remove
bacon and crumble coarsely. Pare potatoes and slice very thin. Add
to bacon drippings in skillet. Sprinkle with salt and pepper. Cook
slowly, turning occasionally, until potatoes are quite brown and
almost tender. Add bacon pieces; cover skillet and cook slowly until
potatoes are tender. Makes 4 to 6 servings.

❀ Fruited Sweet Potatoes

2 (18 oz.) cans vacuum-
    packed sweet potatoes
1 (13½ oz.) can pineapple
    chunks
1 (8 oz.) can sliced
    peaches, drained
2 medium oranges, peeled
    and cut into sections

2 teaspoons grated orange
    peel
2 tablespoons honey
1 teaspoon salt
⅛ teaspoon pepper
2 tablespoons butter or
    margarine

Heat oven to 350°. Arrange sweet potatoes in shallow 1½-quart baking dish. Drain pineapple and reserve juice. Mix pineapple, peaches, and orange sections; spoon over sweet potatoes. Mix orange peel, reserved pineapple juice, honey, salt, and pepper; pour over fruit. Dot top with butter. Bake 25 to 30 minutes, or until thoroughly heated. Makes 6 to 8 servings.

❀ Hot Slaw

1 medium green cabbage
6 slices bacon, coarsely
    chopped
½ teaspoon celery seed

¼ cup brown sugar, packed
½ teaspoon dry mustard
¼ cup vinegar
½ teaspoon salt

Shred the cabbage coarsely. Cook bacon in heavy saucepan over low heat until crisp. Remove bacon pieces and add remaining ingredients, except cabbage, to the bacon drippings. When mixture is hot, add cabbage and toss until well coated. Remove from heat and sprinkle with bacon pieces. Makes 4 servings.

❀ Pineapple-Glazed Beets

3 tablespoons butter or
    margarine
2 tablespoons light-brown
    sugar
½ teaspoon ginger
dash nutmeg

dash salt
1 cup pineapple juice
1 teaspoon lemon juice
2 teaspoons cornstarch
1 (1 lb. 4 oz.) can small
    whole beets, drained

Slowly heat butter in medium saucepan. Add sugar, ginger, nutmeg, and salt, stirring until sugar dissolves. Remove from heat. Add juices, mixing well. Combine a little of juice mixture with cornstarch, stirring to make a smooth paste. Return to saucepan. Cook, stirring constantly, over medium heat until mixture begins to boil and becomes thickened and translucent. Add beets; cook, uncovered, over medium heat, stirring occasionally, until glaze is reduced in volume and just covers beets—about 10 minutes. Serve beets hot, with glaze spooned over. Makes 4 servings.

❁ Red Cabbage

1 (3 lb.) head red cabbage, shredded (12 cups)

3 tart red cooking apples, cored and thinly sliced

2 tablespoons salt

2 tablespoons margarine

½ cup cider vinegar

½ cup sugar

½ cup water

In large skillet combine all ingredients. Cook over medium heat, covered and stirring occasionally, 20 to 25 minutes, or until cabbage is tender but still crisp. Makes 6 servings.

❁ Scalloped Onions and Peppers

10 medium onions, peeled

1 cup small strips green pepper

3 tablespoons butter or margarine

3 tablespoons flour

½ teaspoon salt

1½ cups milk

¼ cup chopped salted peanuts

Cook onions in a large amount of boiling salted water about 10 minutes, or until just tender. Add green pepper strips during the last 5 minutes. Drain and cool slightly. Cut onions into halves or quarters. Arrange onions and green pepper in a buttered, shallow 1½-quart baking dish. Melt butter in a saucepan over low heat. Blend in flour and salt; cook until bubbly. Gradually stir in milk. Cook over moderate heat, stirring constantly, until thickened and smooth. Pour sauce over vegetables in casserole. Sprinkle with chopped peanuts. Heat oven to 350°. Bake 30 to 40 minutes, until bubbly. Makes 6 servings.

❈ *Three Bean Salad*

1 (15½ oz.) can red kidney   ½ cup chopped onion
  beans, drained   ½ cup chopped celery
1 (1 lb.) can green beans,   1 teaspoon salt
  drained   ¼ teaspoon pepper
1 (1 lb.) can wax beans,   ½ cup mayonnaise
  drained   ½ cup ketchup

Combine all ingredients. Chill 2 to 3 hours before serving. Makes
6 to 8 servings.

❈ *Turnips and Onions*

2 pounds turnips   1 chicken bouillon cube
3 cups thinly sliced onion   ½ cup boiling water
salt   2 tablespoons butter or
pepper   margarine

Heat oven to 400°. Pare turnips; cut in half and then into thin crosswise slices. Arrange alternate layers of turnip and onion in a greased
2½-quart casserole. Sprinkle layers lightly with salt and pepper. Dissolve bouillon cube in boiling water and pour over vegetables. Dot
with butter. Cover and bake 1½ hours, or until turnips are fork
tender. Makes 6 servings.

❈ *Western Lima Bake*

1 pound dried lima beans   2 (8 oz.) cans tomato sauce
½ pound ground beef   ½ cup lima cooking liquid
1 medium onion, finely   ½ teaspoon salt
  chopped   dash poultry seasoning
3 tablespoons salad oil

Wash beans and soak overnight in 2 quarts water. Simmer in same
water until tender, 1 to 1½ hours. Season beans with 2½ teaspoons
salt after ½ hour of cooking. Drain and put in casserole, reserving ½
cup lima cooking liquid. Cook meat and onion in hot salad oil, stirring until lightly browned. Add tomato sauce and remaining ingredients. Mix and pour hot sauce over beans. Bake at 350° 1 hour, or
until bubbly hot. Makes 5 to 6 servings.

CASSEROLES

What makes a so-so cook reap after-dinner compliments? keeps the woman confronted with a gaggle of unexpected guests from dashing right out the back door as they enter? gives a mother time to read two chapters of the latest best seller while dinner is cooking? lets the hostess stay in the living room with the guests instead of in the kitchen with the stove? There is only one answer—the Casserole, also known as the One-Dish Meal. Someday a homemaker is going to write a "Hymn to the Casserole" and hit the Top Ten. Every cook in the country would make it her theme song.

One of the most encouraging things about casserole dishes is the fact that it is almost impossible to turn out a bad one. If you don't know how to cook very well, a casserole meal can make you look like a Dione Lucas. If you do know how to cook, casseroles let you indulge your sense of adventure. If you haven't much time, a casserole is again the solution. And if you want to prepare tomorrow's meal today, what else? The casserole, an eminently freezable, reheatable dish.

A casserole can be incredibly versatile. Hearty for the he-men round the table. Elegantly continental for the new neighbors you're trying to impress. Or just plain practical for a Saturday night supper. Economical? Can you think of a better way to use up those odds and ends in the back of the refrigerator or disguise the weekend meat bargain? We are convinced that casseroles belong to the world of legerdemain. They can make things taste like what they're not—better, more flavorful, even more expensive. Stews and other looked-down-on victuals take on a definite sophistication when prepared *en casserole*. The simplest foods—like hamburger, tuna fish, potatoes, or macaroni—eased into a casserole, paired with the right companions, sauces, and seasonings, can emerge, like Cinderella from her pumpkin coach, totally different in character.

If following the budget road has led you straight into mealtime monotony, try including in your menus some of the one-dish recipes that follow. (You will find additional casserole recipes in other chapters.) They are all favorites of ours, fun to prepare and serve and astonishingly economical. Add a green salad, a beverage, and dessert, and your worries are over. Until the next meal, that is.

✿ *Alsatian Pork Chops*

4 *blade pork shoulder chops, 1 inch thick*	1 *(16 oz.) can sauerkraut*
seasoned instant meat tenderizer	½ *teaspoon caraway seeds*
2 *tablespoons shortening*	2 *cooking apples, pared, cored, and sliced*
2 *medium onions, thinly sliced*	¾ *cup water*

Heat oven to 350°. Trim excess fat from chops. Brush surface of chops with water and sprinkle both sides with meat tenderizer. Pierce meat with a fork at ½-inch intervals. Melt shortening in skillet over moderately high heat; cook chops until lightly browned. Remove chops; add onions and cook until tender. Spoon half the sauerkraut into a shallow 2½-quart casserole. Sprinkle with half the caraway seeds. Top with apple slices and onions and sprinkle with the remaining caraway seeds. Spoon remaining sauerkraut over apples. Arrange pork chops over top. Add water to skillet to loosen meat drippings; pour over chops. Cover and bake 1 to 1¼ hours, or until fork tender. Makes 4 servings.

❀ Baked Jambalaya

1½ cups packaged
  precooked rice
2 slices diced bacon
¼ cup finely chopped
  onion
¼ cup chopped green
  pepper
1½ cups tomato juice
1 small (6 oz.) can tomato
  paste
1 cup water

¼ teaspoon paprika
¼ teaspoon dried thyme
  leaves
½ teaspoon sugar
½ teaspoon salt
few grains pepper
2 tablespoons chopped
  parsley
1 cup diced cooked chicken
  or turkey
1 cup diced cooked ham

Heat oven to 350°. Cook rice according to package directions. Cook bacon in skillet until lightly browned. Remove bacon; add onion and green pepper and cook in drippings until tender. Add tomato juice, tomato paste, water, paprika, thyme, sugar, salt, and pepper; heat until blended. Remove from heat. Mix together rice, tomato mixture, parsley, chicken, and ham; pour into greased 1½-quart casserole. Cover and bake 30 to 35 minutes. Makes 6 servings.

❀ Casserole Marie-Blanche

8 ounces noodles, cooked
  and drained
1 cup creamed cottage
  cheese
1 cup commercial sour
  cream

½ teaspoon salt
⅛ teaspoon pepper
⅓ cup chopped chives
1 tablespoon butter or
  margarine

Heat oven to 350°. Combine noodles, cheese, sour cream, salt, pepper, and chives. Pour into a buttered 2-quart casserole and dot top with the 1 tablespoon butter. Bake about 30 minutes, until noodles begin to brown. Serve immediately. Makes 4 servings.

❀ Curried Spaghetti

2 tablespoons butter or
  margarine
1 (4 oz.) can sliced
  mushrooms, drained
1 teaspoon instant minced
  onion
1 (10½ oz.) can condensed
  cream of chicken soup
1 (10½ oz.) can condensed
  cream of celery soup

1½ teaspoons curry powder
1 cup milk
8 ounces spaghetti, cooked
  and drained
2 cups cubed cooked
  chicken or turkey
¼ cup slivered almonds

Heat oven to 350°. Melt butter in skillet over moderately low heat.
Add mushrooms and cook until lightly browned. Remove from heat.
Add onion. Blend in cream of chicken and celery soups, curry, and
milk. Combine sauce with spaghetti and chicken. Pour into but-
tered 2½-quart casserole. Sprinkle with almonds. Bake 35 minutes.
Makes 4 servings.

❀ Easy Spaghetti Bake

2 slices bacon, diced
2 medium onions, chopped
1 clove garlic, minced
½ pound lean ground beef
2½ cups water
2 (8 oz.) cans tomato sauce
1½ teaspoons salt

1 teaspoon chili powder
pepper to taste
½ cup sliced ripe olives
8 ounces spaghetti
1½ cups shredded sharp
  Cheddar cheese

In skillet fry bacon about 2 minutes; add onions and garlic and cook
until soft. Add meat; cook until red color is gone. Stir in water, tomato sauce, salt, chili powder, and pepper. Simmer, covered, 25
minutes; stir in olives. Break half the spaghetti into oiled 2-quart
casserole; cover with half the tomato sauce mixture; sprinkle with
half the cheese; repeat layers. Bake, covered, at 350° for 30 minutes. Uncover, bake 15 minutes longer. Makes 4 servings.

🌸 Egg Salad Casserole

6 hard-cooked eggs,
  chopped
2 tablespoons chopped
  pimiento
½ cup finely chopped
  celery
1½ cups finely crushed pilot
  crackers

1 cup mayonnaise
¼ cup milk
½ teaspoon salt
¼ teaspoon pepper
¾ teaspoon garlic salt
2 tablespoons melted butter
  or margarine

Heat oven to 400°. Mix eggs, pimiento, celery, 1 cup of the crushed crackers, mayonnaise, milk, salt, garlic salt, and pepper. Spread mixture in a greased, shallow 1-quart casserole or a 9-inch pie pan. Toss together the remaining ½ cup of cracker crumbs and butter; sprinkle over egg mixture. Bake about 20 minutes, until lightly browned. Makes 3 to 4 servings.

🌸 Family Salmon Casserole

¼ (1 lb.) package
  spaghetti twists (1¼
  cups)
1 (10 oz.) package frozen
  mixed vegetables
2 (1½ oz.) packages
  à-la-king sauce mix
3 cups milk
1 cup commercial sour
  cream

¼ teaspoon dried dill
1 (1 lb.) can red salmon,
  drained and broken into
  large pieces
2 hard-cooked eggs, cut
  into eighths
1 (1¾ oz.) can potato
  sticks

Preheat oven to 375°. Cook spaghetti and mixed vegetables as package labels direct; drain. Prepare sauce mix as package label directs, using the milk and adding sour cream and dill. Bring just to boil. In 2-quart casserole, combine all the ingredients except the potato sticks. Sprinkle potato sticks over top of casserole. Bake 15 to 20 minutes, or until heated through. Makes 4 servings.

❀ Fish 'n Chips Casserole

4 slices bacon, diced
1 cup chopped onion
½ cup chopped green
  pepper
2 (8 oz.) cans or 1 (15 oz.)
  can tomato sauce with
  tomato bits
1 (12 oz.) can whole kernel
  corn

1¼ teaspoons salt
¼ teaspoon marjoram or
  thyme
1 (14 oz.) package frozen
  fish sticks
1 cup shredded sharp
  Cheddar cheese
1 (9 oz.) package frozen
  French fries, cut in thirds

In skillet cook bacon until lightly browned; add onion and green pepper and cook until vegetables are almost tender. Stir in tomato sauce, corn, 1 teaspoon salt, and marjoram or thyme. Meanwhile, arrange fish sticks in bottom of lightly oiled 2-quart baking dish; sprinkle with ½ cup cheese. Pour on tomato sauce mixture, then top with French fries. Sprinkle with remaining ¼ teaspoon salt. Bake at 375° for 35 minutes. Sprinkle remaining cheese over top; bake 10 minutes more. Makes 4 to 6 servings.

❀ Lima Ham Casserole

2 cups large dried lima
  beans
2 tablespoons butter or
  margarine
1 cup sliced onion
¼ cup chopped green
  pepper
1 pound cooked ham, cut
  into 1-inch cubes

½ cup ketchup
¼ cup molasses
1 tablespoon vinegar
2 teaspoons Worcestershire
  sauce
1½ teaspoons dry mustard

Cook beans as directed on package. Drain and reserve ½ cup of the liquid. Heat oven to 325°. Melt butter in skillet over low heat. Add onion and green pepper; cook until tender. Combine onion mixture with lima beans. Arrange alternate layers of beans and ham in a 2-quart casserole. Combine ketchup, molasses, vinegar, Worcestershire, and mustard with the reserved ½ cup bean liquid. Pour over beans. Bake about 45 minutes, until most of the liquid is absorbed; stir twice during baking. Makes 4 servings.

❀ *Macaroni-Chili Casserole*

2 slices bacon, cut up
1½ pounds beef chuck or
   rump, cut in ½-inch
   cubes
1 cup sliced onion
1 (1 pt. 2 oz.) can tomato
   juice

1 (1¼ oz.) package chili-
   seasoning mix
1 (15 oz.) can red kidney
   beans, with liquid
8 ounces elbow macaroni
½ cup grated Cheddar
   cheese

In Dutch oven fry bacon pieces until crisp. Remove pieces; reserve. Add beef and onion to bacon fat and sauté until well browned—about 15 minutes. Add the tomato juice and chili-seasoning mix; bring to boil. Reduce heat and simmer, covered, stirring occasionally, 1 hour, or until beef is tender. Add kidney beans; simmer 15 minutes longer. Meanwhile, cook macaroni as package label directs; drain. Stir into beef mixture with bacon. Turn into 2½-quart casserole; sprinkle with cheese. Broil 4 inches from heat until cheese melts. Makes 4 servings.

❀ *Mandarin Lamb Casserole*

4 thick shoulder lamb chops
salt
pepper
1 cup uncooked rice
1 (11 oz.) can mandarin
   orange sections

2½ cups boiling water
3 chicken bouillon cubes
½ teaspoon dried mint
   leaves

Heat oven to 325°. Remove pieces of fat from chops and heat in a heavy skillet over moderate heat (about 250°) until fat melts. Brown chops quickly in fat over higher heat (about 350°). Season with salt and pepper. Place rice in bottom of a greased shallow 2-quart casserole. Arrange chops on rice. Drain oranges. Measure syrup from oranges and add enough boiling water to make 3 cups. Add bouillon cubes; stir to dissolve. Arrange orange sections on chops. Pour in liquid mixture and sprinkle with mint. Cover; bake 1½ hours, until chops and rice are tender. Makes 4 servings.

🌼 *Moussaka*

1 *pound ground lean lamb*	1 *(16 oz.) can tomatoes*
salt	½ *cup fine dry bread*
pepper	*crumbs*
1 *medium eggplant, peeled*	½ *cup grated Parmesan*
and thinly sliced	*cheese*

Heat oven to 400°. Combine lamb, salt, and pepper. Arrange a layer of lamb in the bottom of a shallow 2-quart casserole. Add a layer of eggplant and some of the tomatoes. Repeat layers, ending with eggplant. Sprinkle top with bread crumbs and then Parmesan cheese. Bake 35 to 40 minutes. Makes 4 servings.

🌼 *Noodle Soufflé Casserole*

1 *pound broad noodles*	1 *large onion, finely*
1 *(8 oz.) package cream*	*chopped*
cheese, softened	4 *eggs, well beaten*
¼ *cup soft butter or*	1 *teaspoon salt*
margarine	¼ *teaspoon pepper*
3 *cups commercial sour*	
cream	

Heat oven to 350°. Cook noodles in boiling salted water as directed on package; drain well. Combine cream cheese and butter and beat until creamy. Stir in sour cream and onion. Fold mixture into noodles. Combine eggs, salt, and pepper; gently stir into noodles. Pour into greased, deep 3-quart casserole. Bake about 45 minutes, until top is golden brown. Makes 6 to 8 servings.

🌼 *Pastiche*

1 *pound elbow macaroni*	1 *pound ground beef*
½ *cup butter or margarine*	*(chuck)*
1 *cup grated Parmesan*	1 *teaspoon salt*
cheese	1 *teaspoon oregano*
¼ *cup olive oil*	4 *eggs*
¼ *cup chopped onion*	1 *tablespoon flour*
4 *cloves garlic, mashed*	½ *cup milk*

Cook macaroni in boiling salted water as directed on package.

Drain well. Melt ¼ cup of the butter in a skillet and cook over moderate heat until butter begins to brown. Add to macaroni with Parmesan cheese; mix thoroughly. Heat oven to 300°. Melt remaining ¼ cup butter in a skillet over moderate heat; add olive oil. Add onion and garlic; cook until onion is golden brown. Add meat; cook and stir until meat is browned. Add salt and oregano. Combine meat mixture with macaroni. Pour into greased 3-quart casserole. Beat eggs with flour and milk until mixture is well blended. Pour over meat and macaroni mixture in casserole. Bake 30 minutes. Makes 6 servings.

❊ Scalloped Sausage Casserole

6 *cups thinly sliced raw potatoes*
⅔ *cup finely chopped onion*
1½ *cups finely chopped celery*
1 *(8 oz.) package brown-and-serve sausages, cut in half*

½ *teaspoon salt*
⅛ *teaspoon pepper*
1 *can condensed cream of celery soup*
1 *soup can milk*
3 *tablespoons butter or margarine*

Heat oven to 375°. Arrange alternate layers of potatoes, onion, celery, sausages, and seasonings in a greased 2½-quart casserole. Pour combined soup and milk over potatoes. Dot with butter. Cover and bake for 1¼ hours. Uncover and bake about 30 minutes longer, or until potatoes are tender and browned on top. Makes 6 servings.

❊ Meat and Vegetable Pie

¼ *cup chopped onion*
4 *tablespoons salad oil*
1½ *teaspoons salt*
¼ *teaspoon pepper*
2 *tablespoons flour*
2 *cups cubed leftover meat*
3 *cups cooked mixed vegetables*

2 *(8 oz.) cans tomato sauce*
1¼ *cups beef bouillon*
1 *tablespoon Worcestershire sauce*
biscuit dough (2-cup recipe)

Brown onion in salad oil. Stir in salt, pepper, and flour. Heat. Add the meat and vegetables, tomato sauce, bouillon, and Worcester-

shire. Heat thoroughly and pour into 2-quart casserole. Roll biscuit
dough ¼ inch thick for top crust, or cover filling with 2-inch biscuits. Bake in 425° oven for 20 minutes, or until top is golden brown.
Makes 5 to 6 servings.

✾ "Sloppy Joe" Casserole

1 (8 oz.) package shell macaroni	*1 (6 oz.) can tomato paste*
1 (1⁵⁄₁₆ oz.) envelope "Sloppy Joe" seasoning mix	*1 (8 oz.) can tomato sauce with cheese*
1 pound ground beef (chuck)	*2 (8 oz.) cartons creamed cottage cheese*
	½ cup grated sharp Cheddar cheese

Cook macaroni as package label directs; drain. Meanwhile, prepare seasoning mix with ground chuck, tomato paste, tomato sauce,
and 1½ cups water as package label directs. Preheat oven to 350°.
In 2½-quart casserole, layer half the macaroni, half the cottage
cheese, and half the meat sauce; repeat. Top with Cheddar cheese.
Bake, uncovered, 40 to 50 minutes, or until bubbling. Makes 4
servings.

✾ Spanish Chicken Casserole

1 (3 lb.) frying chicken, cut up	*2 cups water*
salt	*1 teaspoon salt*
pepper	*¼ teaspoon pepper*
¼ cup salad oil	*1 cup raw rice*
½ cup chopped onion	*1 (10 oz.) package frozen peas, thawed*
2 (8 oz.) cans tomato sauce with mushrooms	*½ cup sliced ripe olives*

Sprinkle chicken with salt and pepper; brown in salad oil in skillet.
Add onion and sauté. Stir in tomato sauce, water, salt, pepper, and
rice. Bring to boil; cover and simmer 45 minutes. Add peas and
olives; continue cooking, covered, 15 minutes. Makes 4 to 5 servings.

❁ Sweet Potato and Sausage Casserole

4 *large sweet potatoes*
(about 3 lbs.)
1 *pound bulk sausage meat*
salt
1 *(8½ oz.) can sliced*
pineapple, drained and
cut in half

2 *tablespoons dark-brown*
sugar
2 *tablespoons melted butter*
2 *tablespoons light cream*
¼ *cup dark-brown sugar,*
firmly packed

Wash potatoes and place in saucepan with boiling water to cover. Cover pan and cook over moderate heat about 30 minutes, or until just tender. Remove, cool, and peel. Slice into ½-inch crosswise slices. Heat oven to 350°. Shape sausage meat into 6 patties about ½ inch thick. Cook in skillet over moderate heat until lightly browned on both sides. Place half of potatoes in layer in bottom of a shallow 1½-quart baking dish; sprinkle lightly with salt. Place sausage patties over potatoes for second layer. Place pineapple over sausage patties. Sprinkle lightly with salt and the 2 tablespoons brown sugar. Top with remaining potato slices. Brush with melted butter and cream. Sprinkle with ¼ cup brown sugar. Bake 45 minutes. Makes 4 servings.

❁ Sweet Potato-Pork Chop Casserole

3 *large sweet potatoes,*
peeled
2 *tablespoons melted butter*
or margarine
2 *tablespoons brown sugar*
3 *tart apples, pared and*
sliced
1 *large sweet onion, thinly*
sliced

4 *shoulder pork chops, cut*
about 1½ inches thick
2 *tablespoons butter or*
margarine
2 *tablespoons flour*
1 *teaspoon salt*
1 *cup beer*

Slice sweet potatoes into a greased 3-quart casserole. Sprinkle with the melted butter and sugar. Arrange apples and onions over potatoes. Top with lightly browned chops. Heat oven to 350°. Melt the 2 tablespoons butter in saucepan over moderate heat. Stir in flour and salt. Gradually add beer; cook and stir until thickened. Pour

sauce over chops. Cover and bake 1¼ hours. Remove cover; bake
30 minutes longer. Makes 4 servings.

❀ *Tuna Cashew Casserole*

*1 (3 oz.) can chow mein
noodles*
*1 can condensed cream of
mushroom soup*
¼ cup water
1 (7 oz.) can tuna, drained
*¾ cup chopped salted
cashew nuts*

⅓ cup diced celery
¼ cup minced onion
¼ cup chopped ripe olives
½ teaspoon salt
few grains pepper

Heat oven to 350°. Reserve ¾ cup of the noodles. Combine rest of
noodles and remaining ingredients. Pour into greased 1½-quart
casserole. Sprinkle with reserved noodles. Bake 40 minutes. Makes
4 servings.

DESSERTS

It is an accepted fact that a great many people (present company included) wade through meals merely to get to the dessert. For some it may be a sweet tooth, for others a childhood conditioning. ("You won't get any cake unless you eat all your vegetables!") But whatever the attitude toward them, desserts can make or break a meal. If the dessert is a delight, the underdone roast will be forgiven. If it's a disappointment, it will discredit the most delectable entree.

The quickest, safest, and least expensive dessert (and an attractive one) is a bowl of fruit in season. Particularly after a hearty meal this is a sane choice. Crackers and an assortment of cheese are also a faultless dessert and certainly one to eliminate hostess fatigue. And for sheer popularity, who can gainsay ice cream? Try serving a bowl full of scoops of various ice creams plus an assortment of toppings and let everyone make his own dessert. The family will love it.

Still, there are many occasions that call for a "real" dessert—something that testifies to skill, creativity, and concern on the cook's part. This is when the budget-watcher is put to the test—heavy cream, raspberries out of season, and rich pastries can be expensive. The trick is to accomplish the same results with less costly ingredients. Medium cream whips as well as heavy, canned fruit can replace the fresh fruit flown in from distant places with a high price tag on its basket. And there are many budget ingredients that can be used to achieve tantalizing party-type desserts. Gelatin for one, bread for another. Many people think a good bread pudding has as much glamour as a diamond necklace. And graham cracker pie crusts are the cook's special blessing.

When talking about expense-paring in the food department, these questions often arise: Are packaged cake mixes truly economical? Would it be just as cheap to buy a ready-made cake? When should one start from scratch to make a cake?

Ready-to-serve and frozen cakes cost more than recipe cakes made at home, but some cakes made from mixes cost about the same as, and, in some cases, less than the recipe cake. Cake mixes (and frozen pies), luxuries at their regular prices, often drop in price when featured as weekend specials. Watch for them and also for introductions of new-flavor cake mixes. Manufacturers often introduce new types of cake mixes at very substantial reductions.

The busy housewife should consider the fact that cake mixes save her time and labor, thus offsetting any extra pennies spent. But totally *verboten* are ready-made frostings. They are an out-and-out luxury. Make your own and save as much as 50 percent of their cost. Recipe cakes? Make them when you happen to have all the ingredients at hand *and* the time. Or when your mother-in-law is coming to dinner.

Put your refrigerator or freezer to work at dessert time as often as possible. There are scores of frozen desserts (several are included here) that are easy to make, economical, and extremely popular with young and old. Frozen desserts are always a fairly safe choice if the hostess is not sure of her guests' preferences.

Be it fruit, cheese, or ice cream; pie, cake, pudding, or frozen goody, we recommend that the dessert be served as a dramatic finale to your meal on your prettiest dishes. In fact, all food, but especially budget meals that might have an element of sparse simplicity about them, should be presented with flair—on fine china or bright pottery, surrounded by colorful place mats, napkins, and fresh flowers whenever possible. Imaginative cooks as well as makeup artists know that camouflage can work wonders.

❀ Apples 'n Custard

1 cup milk	½ teaspoon vanilla extract
2 egg yolks	1 (1 lb. 4 oz.) can apple
3 tablespoons granulated	slices
sugar	½ cup granulated sugar
dash salt	2 tablespoons lemon juice

First make a custard sauce. Heat milk in top of double boiler over direct heat until bubbles form around the edge of the pan. In small bowl, slightly beat egg yolks with 3 tablespoons granulated sugar and the salt. Gradually add hot milk, stirring constantly. Return to double boiler top. Cook, stirring constantly, over simmering water until mixture coats a metal spoon. Stir in vanilla. Pour into small bowl. Refrigerate, covered, until chilled. Meanwhile, drain apple slices well; discard liquid. Place slices in medium saucepan. Stir in ½ cup granulated sugar and the lemon juice. Heat to boil, reduce heat; cook, uncovered and stirring once or twice, 20 minutes, or until apples are glazed and liquid has evaporated. Keep warm. To serve, spoon warm apple slices into dessert dishes, pour chilled custard over each serving. Top with whipped cream, if desired. Makes 4 servings.

❀ Apricot Pandowdy

1 (1 lb. 1 oz.) can unpeeled apricot halves	1 (9 oz.) package one-layer yellow cake mix
1 tablespoon cornstarch	1 teaspoon vanilla extract
1 teaspoon grated lemon peel	¾ cup light cream

Preheat oven to 350°. Grease a 1½-quart casserole. Drain apricots; reserve liquid. Gradually stir liquid into cornstarch in small bowl; add lemon peel and apricots. Pour into prepared casserole. Prepare cake mix as package label directs, adding vanilla with liquid called for on package. Carefully pour over apricot mixture. Bake 40 to 45 minutes, or until top is golden brown and springs back when gently pressed with fingertip. Spoon into serving dishes. Serve warm, with cream. Makes 6 servings.

❀ Banana and Bread Custard

4 tablespoons soft butter or margarine	2 medium bananas, sliced
6 slices day-old white bread	4 eggs
⅔ cup granulated sugar	2 cups milk
1 teaspoon cinnamon	1 teaspoon vanilla extract
	3 tablespoons brown sugar

Preheat oven to 350°. Spread 1 tablespoon butter over bottom and side of 1½-quart baking dish. Trim crusts from bread. Spread slices with remaining butter; sprinkle with 3 tablespoons granulated sugar and the cinnamon. Cut into ½-inch cubes. Arrange half of bread in prepared baking dish; top with half of banana slices. Add remaining bread and top with remaining banana slices. In medium bowl combine eggs, milk, vanilla, and remaining granulated sugar; mix until well blended. Pour over bread and bananas. Set baking dish in shallow baking pan; pour hot water to 1-inch depth around dish. Bake 45 minutes. Sprinkle brown sugar over top; bake 10 to 15 minutes, or until knife inserted in center comes out clean. Let cool on wire rack about 20 minutes. Serve warm. Makes 8 servings.

✿ Black Bottom Pie

1 9-inch pastry shell
1 (1 oz.) square unsweetened chocolate
1 (4 serving) package chocolate pudding and pie mix
1¾ cups milk
½ teaspoon vanilla extract

1 (3½ oz.) package vanilla-flavor whipped dessert mix
¾ cup light cream
¼ cup chilled light rum
1 cup frozen whipped topping, thawed

Bake and cool pie shell. Melt the chocolate in small saucepan over low heat. Prepare chocolate pudding according to package directions, using only the 1¾ cups milk. Stir melted chocolate and vanilla extract into pudding. Cool, stirring occasionally, until pudding no longer steams. Pour into the cooled pie shell and cool thoroughly. Combine whipped dessert mix and ½ cup of the light cream in small bowl of electric mixer. Whip at highest speed about 1 minute, until very thick. Blend in the remaining ¼ cup light cream and the rum; whip at highest speed about 2 minutes. Fold in the whipped topping. Pour the mixture over the cooled chocolate layer. Chill 2 to 3 hours, or until firm. If desired, garnish with additional whipped topping and chocolate sprinkles. Makes 6 to 8 servings.

❀ Cheesecake

2 cups packaged graham
   cracker crumbs
½ cup melted butter or
   margarine
1 cup sugar
1 (4 serving) package
   lemon-flavored gelatin

1 cup boiling water
2 (3 oz.) packages cream
   cheese, softened to room
   temperature
1 cup sugar
1 (14 oz.) can sweetened
   condensed milk

Combine graham cracker crumbs, butter, and 1 cup sugar in medium-sized bowl and stir to blend well. Reserve ¾ cup of the mixture for topping. Press the remaining cracker mixture on bottom and sides of a shallow 2-quart baking dish. Pour gelatin into small bowl; add boiling water and stir until gelatin is dissolved. Cool; chill until mixture is the consistency of unbeaten egg white. Meanwhile, place cream cheese in the small bowl of an electric mixer and beat until creamy. Gradually add the remaining 1 cup sugar and beat until fluffy. Add sweetened condensed milk slowly and blend well until smooth. Gently fold cheese mixture into the gelatin until well blended. Pour into prepared dish. Sprinkle the reserved crumbs on top. Chill 3 hours. Cut into squares to serve. Makes 9 to 12 servings.

❀ Chocolate Blancmange

2 cups milk
2 (1 oz.) squares
   unsweetened chocolate
3 tablespoons cornstarch

⅛ teaspoon salt
¼ cup sugar
½ teaspoon vanilla extract

Combine 1½ cups milk and the chocolate; heat in top of double boiler until chocolate is melted. Beat with rotary beater until smooth. Mix cornstarch, salt, sugar, and the remaining ½ cup milk; stir slowly into the hot milk. Cook over boiling water 10 minutes, stirring constantly, until smooth and thickened. Cover and continue to cook 15 minutes, stirring occasionally. Remove from heat; stir in vanilla. Turn into individual molds that have been rinsed with cold water. Chill blancmange for 1 hour, until firm. Unmold onto chilled serving dishes and serve with plain or whipped cream. Makes 4 to 6 servings.

❀ Cocoa Freeze

¾ cup undiluted
   evaporated milk
⅓ cup sugar
2 tablespoons cocoa

2 tablespoons flour
¼ cup milk
¼ cup water
½ teaspoon vanilla extract

Pour evaporated milk into a bowl. Put it into refrigerator along with a rotary beater to chill thoroughly. Combine sugar, cocoa, and flour. Combine milk and water; gradually stir into cocoa mixture. Place over low heat; bring to a boil and cook, stirring, about 3 minutes, until slightly thickened. Add vanilla. Chill thoroughly. Whip the chilled milk with the chilled beater until stiff. Fold milk into chilled cocoa mixture. Pour into a freezer tray and freeze without stirring in freezer compartment. Makes 1 quart.

❀ Coconut Bread Pudding

1½ cups cubed day-old
   bread
3 cups milk, scalded
2 eggs, well beaten

½ cup sugar
¼ teaspoon salt
½ teaspoon cinnamon
½ cup flaked coconut

Heat oven to 350°. Butter a 1½-quart casserole. Put bread cubes in casserole. Pour in milk. Combine eggs, sugar, salt, cinnamon, and coconut. Add to bread cubes and stir until blended. Set casserole in a large pan and pour hot water into the pan to a depth of 1 inch. Bake 45 to 50 minutes, until a silver knife inserted in center comes out clean. Makes 6 servings.

❀ Coffee Whip

1 tablespoon unflavored
   gelatin
¼ cup cold water

2 cups strong hot coffee
6 tablespoons sugar
½ teaspoon vanilla extract

Sprinkle gelatin over water to soften. Add hot coffee and stir until gelatin is dissolved. Stir in sugar and vanilla. Chill until almost firm. Whip with rotary beater until light and fluffy. Spoon into serving dishes and chill until firm. Serve with cream if desired. Makes 6 servings.

❈ *Cranberry Betty*

1 cup sugar
½ cup orange juice
½ teaspoon cinnamon
2 cups fresh cranberries

½ cup melted butter or
   margarine
3 cups soft bread crumbs

Heat oven to 375°. Combine sugar, orange juice, and cinnamon in a small saucepan. Bring to boil over moderate heat, add cranberries and cook uncovered 2 minutes, until berries pop. Add butter to bread crumbs and toss to coat evenly. Arrange alternate layers of buttered crumbs and cranberries in a buttered 2-quart casserole, starting and ending with crumbs. Cover and bake 20 minutes. Remove cover and bake about 15 minutes longer, until top is brown and crisp. Makes 6 to 8 servings.

❈ *Creamy Rice Pudding*

4 cups milk
¼ cup uncooked rice
¼ cup sugar

½ teaspoon salt
½ teaspoon vanilla extract

Heat oven to 325°. Heat milk to the boiling point. Combine rice, sugar, and salt in a buttered 1½-quart casserole. Pour hot milk over rice, add vanilla, and stir well. Bake 1½ hours. A brown crust will form during baking; stir this in every 20 minutes during first hour of baking. During last half hour allow top to brown slightly. Chill before serving. Makes 4 to 6 servings.

❀ Crispy Chocolate Sticks

COOKY LAYER:

1 square unsweetened
  chocolate
¼ cup butter or
  margarine
1 egg

½ cup granulated sugar
¼ cup sifted all-purpose
  flour
¼ cup chopped pecans

FILLING:

2 tablespoons soft butter
  or margarine
1 cup confectioners' sugar

1 tablespoon heavy cream
  or evaporated milk
¼ teaspoon vanilla extract

GLAZE:

1 square unsweetened
  chocolate

1 tablespoon butter or
  margarine

COOKY LAYER: Preheat oven to 350°. Grease an 8 by 8 by 2 inch pan. Melt chocolate and butter together over hot water. Cool slightly. In medium bowl beat egg till frothy. Stir in chocolate mixture and sugar. Add flour and nuts, stirring until well blended. Turn into prepared pan; bake 20 minutes. Cool thoroughly on wire rack.

FILLING: In small bowl, blend all ingredients. Spread over cooky layer. Chill at least 10 minutes.

Glaze with the chocolate and butter after melting them over hot water. Refrigerate 15 minutes to harden glaze. With sharp knife, cut into 18 sticks.

❀ Double Fudge Torte

1 (1 lb.) package fudge
  brownie mix
2 eggs
1 (3¾ oz.) package
  chocolate-fudge-flavor
  whipped dessert mix

½ teaspoon cinnamon
½ cup cold milk
1 (⅞ oz.) milk chocolate
  candy bar

Preheat oven to 350°. Grease two 8-inch layer-cake pans. Line with waxed paper; grease paper. Prepare brownie mix with 2 eggs as package label directs for cakelike brownies. Turn into prepared pans. Bake 25 minutes. Let cool in pans on wire rack 10 minutes. Remove from pans; let cool completely. Meanwhile, combine dessert mix and cinnamon. Prepare with cold milk and ½ cup water as package directs. Refrigerate until chilled. Beat chilled pudding until smooth. Spread on top of both brownie layers; stack layers. Cut chocolate bar into triangles, stand in circle on top of torte. Refrigerate several hours before serving. Makes 6 servings.

❀ French Apple Cobbler

FILLING:

5 cups pared, cored, and sliced tart apples
¾ cup sugar
2 tablespoons all-purpose flour
½ teaspoon cinnamon

¼ teaspoon salt
1 teaspoon vanilla extract
¼ cup water
1 tablespoon soft butter or margarine

BATTER:

½ cup sifted all-purpose flour
½ cup sugar
½ teaspoon baking powder

¼ teaspoon salt
2 tablespoons soft butter or margarine
1 egg, slightly beaten

Preheat oven to 375°. *Make Filling first:* In medium bowl combine apples, sugar, flour, cinnamon, salt, vanilla, and water. Turn into a 9 by 9 by 1¾″ baking pan. Dot apples with butter.

BATTER: In medium bowl, combine all batter ingredients; beat with wooden spoon until smooth. Drop batter in 9 portions on apples, spacing evenly; batter will spread during baking. Bake 35 to 40 minutes, or until apples are fork tender and crust is golden brown. Serve warm, with light or whipped cream if desired. Makes 6 to 8 servings.

❀ *Frozen Coffee Custard*

1 egg, separated
¼ cup sugar
2 teaspoons instant coffee
  powder

½ teaspoon vanilla extract
1 (6 oz.) can evaporated
  milk, chilled ice-cold

Beat egg yolk. Add sugar, instant coffee, and vanilla. Beat until sugar is dissolved. Beat egg white until stiff but not dry. Fold into yolk mixture. Whip milk until very stiff. Gently fold egg mixture into whipped milk. Turn at once into a chilled aluminum loaf pan or freezer trays. Cover tightly with aluminum foil. Freeze until solid. Makes about 1 pint. Frozen custard is best when served same day it is made.

❀ *Lemon-Drop Sherbet*

2 teaspoons unflavored
  gelatin
1⅓ cups sugar
7 tablespoons nonfat dry
  milk solids
1 cup water

1 teaspoon grated lemon
  peel
1 cup lemon juice
1 egg white
2 tablespoons sugar

Combine gelatin, the 1⅓ cups sugar, and the dry milk solids in a saucepan; gradually stir in the water. Place over moderately low heat and heat about 5 minutes, or until sugar is dissolved. Cool. Stir in lemon peel and juice. Pour into a 9 by 5 by 2¾ inch loaf pan and place in freezer compartment for about 1 hour, or until sherbet is partially frozen. Beat egg white with rotary beater until soft peaks form. Gradually add the 2 tablespoons sugar and beat until stiff peaks form again. Spoon partially frozen sherbet into a chilled bowl and beat with a rotary beater until smooth. Fold meringue into sherbet and pour back into loaf pan. Freeze 3 to 4 hours, until firm. Serve with touch of crème de menthe or sauce of your choice. Makes 8 servings.

❀ Lemon Fluff Pie

1 cup sugar
¼ cup flour
⅛ teaspoon salt
¾ cup hot water
¼ cup lemon juice
1 egg, slightly beaten
3 tablespoons butter or
  margarine, melted
½ teaspoon grated lemon
  rind

½ cup nonfat dry milk
  solids
½ cup cold water
1 tablespoon lemon juice
¼ teaspoon vanilla extract
1 9-inch pastry shell, baked
  and cooled

Combine sugar, flour, and salt in top of double boiler. Combine hot water and the ¼ cup lemon juice; gradually add to sugar mixture. Stir until smooth and well blended. Place over boiling water; cook, stirring constantly, until mixture is smooth and thickened. Combine a little of the thickened mixture with the beaten egg, then add egg to rest of hot mixture. Continue to cook and stir about 2 minutes, until thickened. Remove from heat and stir in butter and lemon rind. Cover and chill thoroughly. Combine dry milk solids, ½ cup cold water, 1 tablespoon lemon juice, and vanilla in a bowl. With rotary beater whip until stiff. With spatula gently fold whipped milk into chilled custard. Pour into baked pastry shell. Chill 1 hour. Makes 6 servings.

❀ Mexican Pudding

2 (14 oz.) cans sweetened
  condensed milk
¾ teaspoon rum extract
1 pint frozen whipped
  topping, thawed

1 (16 oz.) can sliced
  pineapple, drained
3 tablespoons slivered
  almonds

Place unopened cans of condensed milk in a saucepan; add boiling water to cover. Cover pan and cook over moderately low heat (about 225°) 1½ hours. Remove cans from water; cool and chill several hours. Stir rum extract into whipped topping. Place a pineapple slice in bottom of each individual dessert dish. Open cans of milk and spoon pudding over pineapple slices. Add a spoonful of whipped topping and a garnish of almonds. Makes 8 to 10 servings.

❀ Orange Meringue Pie

FILLING:

1 9-inch pie shell, baked	1½ cups orange juice
7 tablespoons cornstarch	½ cup lemon juice
1 cup sugar	3 egg yolks, slightly beaten
¼ teaspoon salt	1 tablespoon butter or
1 teaspoon grated orange peel	margarine
1 teaspoon grated lemon peel	

MERINGUE:

3 egg whites	2 tablespoons flaked coconut
6 tablespoons sugar	
dash salt	

Prepare pie shell from your favorite recipe or a mix.

FILLING: In top of double boiler combine cornstarch, sugar, and salt. Gradually stir in peels and juices until smooth. Place over boiling water; cook, stirring constantly, 5 minutes. Quickly beat small amount of hot fruit mixture into egg yolks. Return fruit-yolk mixture to top of double boiler, with butter; cook, stirring constantly, 5 minutes. Remove from boiling water; cool completely. Pour into pie shell. Meanwhile, preheat oven to 350°.

MERINGUE: In medium bowl, beat egg whites with rotary beater until soft peaks form when beater is raised. Gradually beat in sugar and salt until stiff peaks form when beater is raised. Spread meringue over pie filling, sealing carefully to rim of shell. Sprinkle with coconut; bake 10 to 15 minutes. Cool completely, away from drafts. Makes 6 servings.

❀ Party Baked Apples

8 medium baking apples	few grains salt
½ cup currant jelly	½ cup sugar
4 egg whites	¼ cup slivered almonds

Heat oven to 375°. Wash and core apples. Starting at stem end, pare apples down about 1 inch. Spoon 1 tablespoon currant jelly into each apple. Bake 35 minutes. Remove from oven and cool 15 minutes. Reduce oven temperature to 325°. Beat egg whites and salt together with rotary beater until soft peaks form. Gradually add sugar and beat until stiff peaks form again. Spread meringue over entire apple; meringue should be about ¾ inch thick. Stud meringue with almonds. Bake 15 minutes, or until meringue is lightly browned. Serve apples at room temperature. Makes 8 servings.

✿ *Peach Pandowdy*

½ cup butter or margarine
½ cup light-brown sugar, firmly packed
1 (1 lb. 1 oz.) can sliced peaches, drained
1½ cups packaged biscuit mix

⅔ cup granulated sugar
¼ cup soft shortening
1 egg
⅔ cup milk
1 teaspoon vanilla extract

Preheat oven to 350°. Put butter in an 8 by 8 by 2 inch pan; place in oven just until butter is melted. Sprinkle brown sugar over butter; arrange peach slices over sugar. In large bowl, combine biscuit mix and granulated sugar. Add shortening, blend in with back of spoon. Add egg, ⅓ cup milk, and vanilla. Beat 1 minute. Gradually beat in remaining milk; continue beating ½ minute longer. Spread evenly over peaches. Bake 40 to 45 minutes, or until cake springs back when gently pressed with fingertip. Let stand in pan on wire rack. Serve warm with whipped cream, if desired. Makes 9 servings.

✿ *Pineapple Cake Roll*

1 (1 lb. 4½ oz.) can crushed pineapple
⅔ cup brown sugar, firmly packed
4 eggs, separated
¼ cup sugar
½ teaspoon vanilla extract
½ cup sugar
¾ cup sifted all-purpose flour

1 teaspoon baking powder
½ teaspoon salt
confectioners' sugar, sifted
3 tablespoons sugar
1½ tablespoons cornstarch
1 cup reserved pineapple juice
⅔ cup orange juice

Heat oven to 375°. Drain pineapple and reserve juice. Spread pineapple evenly on bottom of an ungreased 15½ by 10½ by 1 inch jelly-roll pan. Sprinkle brown sugar over pineapple. Beat egg yolks until thick and lemon colored. Gradually beat in the ¼ cup sugar. Add vanilla. Beat egg whites until soft peaks form; gradually add the ½ cup sugar and continue beating until stiff peaks form. Fold yolk mixture into beaten egg whites. Sift together flour, baking powder, and salt. Fold gently into egg mixture. Spread batter evenly over pineapple in pan. Bake about 20 minutes. Turn cake out onto towel sprinkled with sifted confectioners' sugar. Wrap in the sugared towel and cool. Combine the 3 tablespoons sugar and cornstarch in a saucepan. Gradually stir in the 1 cup reserved pineapple juice and the orange juice. Cook over moderate heat, stirring constantly, until thickened and clear. Serve sauce warm or chilled over slices of cake roll. Makes 8 servings.

❀ *Queen of Puddings*

3 slices white bread
2 eggs, separated
2 cups milk
¼ cup brown sugar, packed
¼ teaspoon salt
2 tablespoons melted butter
* or margarine*

1 teaspoon vanilla extract
2 cups seedless raisins
¼ cup sugar
¼ cup jellied cranberry
* sauce*

Heat oven to 350°. Cut bread into ¼-inch cubes. Beat egg yolks slightly in a medium-sized bowl. Add milk, brown sugar, salt, butter, and vanilla; blend thoroughly. Stir in bread cubes and raisins. Pour mixture into a greased 8-inch square baking dish. Set dish in a larger pan and fill pan with hot water to a depth of 1 inch. Bake 50 minutes. Remove pudding from oven and turn oven regulator to 425°. Beat egg whites until foamy; gradually add the ¼ cup sugar and whip until stiff peaks form. Spread top of pudding with the cranberry sauce. Spoon meringue around edge. Replace pudding in pan of hot water and bake about 5 minutes, until meringue is brown. Serve warm or chilled. Makes 4 servings.

❀ *Spicy Cooky Kisses*

1 cup sifted all-purpose
  flour
⅛ teaspoon baking soda
⅛ teaspoon nutmeg

1 teaspoon cinnamon
¼ cup soft butter or
  margarine
1 cup sugar

Preheat oven to 400°. Sift flour with baking soda, nutmeg, and cinnamon; set aside. In large bowl of electric mixer, at medium speed, beat butter with sugar until very light and fluffy. At low speed beat in flour mixture just until well combined. On lightly floured surface, roll dough ¼ inch thick. Using 2-inch star and heart-shaped cooky cutters, cut out dough. Reroll and cut out leftover dough. Place on ungreased cooky sheets, 1½ inches apart; bake 8 to 10 minutes. Remove from oven; let stand on cooky sheets about 2 minutes. Remove to wire rack. Makes about 4 dozen. Delicious served with coffee ice cream.

❀ *Tutti-Frutti Pudding-Cake*

½ cup apricot preserves
½ cup cherry preserves
1 (1 lb. 2½ oz.) package
  yellow cake mix
2 eggs
1 cup water

½ cup orange juice
1 tablespoon grated orange
  peel
sweetened whipped cream
  or vanilla ice cream

Preheat oven to 350°. Grease and flour 2½-quart pudding mold with tube or 9-inch tube pan. Combine preserves and spoon into bottom of mold. Prepare cake mix with 2 eggs, 1 cup water, and the orange juice as package label directs. Stir in orange peel. Pour into prepared mold. Bake 1¼ hours, or until cake tester comes out clean. Let stand in pan on wire rack 10 minutes. Loosen around edge with small spatula; then invert onto serving plate. Preserves will run down sides of cake as a glaze. Serve warm, with sweetened whipped cream or vanilla ice cream. Makes 8 to 10 servings.

INDEX